Dancer's Guide to Injuries of the Lower Extremity

Dancer's Guide to Injuries of the Lower Extremity

DIAGNOSIS, TREATMENT, AND CARE

Stuart Wright, M.A.ED., M.A.
F.S.C.Ch. (Brit.), M.B.Ch.A.

With a Foreword by
William G. Hamilton, M.D.

Cornwall Books
New York • London • Toronto

© 1985 by Rosemont Publishing and Printing Corporation

Cornwall Books
440 Forsgate Drive
Cranbury, NJ 08512

Cornwall Books
25 Sicilian Avenue
London WC1A 2QH, England

Cornwall Books
2133 Royal Windsor Drive
Unit 1
Mississauga, Ontario
Canada L5J 1K5

Library of Congress Cataloging in Publication Data

Wright, Stuart, 1948—
    Dancer's guide to injuries of the lower extremity.

    Includes index.
    1. Extremities, Lower—Wounds and injuries.
2. Extremities, Lower—Care and hygiene.   3. Dancers—
Health and hygiene.   I. Title.
RD560.W75   1985   617'.57044   84-45008
ISBN 0-8453-4782-9

Printed in the United States of America

To Bobby Lindgren,
who made this book possible

Modicae fidei, quare dubitasti? *The Vulgate*

Es ist Arznei, nicht Gift, was ich dir reiche.
Gotthold Ephraim Lessing

La bonne grâce est au corps ce que le bon sens est à l'esprit.
La Rochefoucauld

I said my prayers devoutly and ate hominy. . . . I danced my
dance. *William Byrd of Westover, 3 April 1709*

Jamque opus exegi, quod nec Jovis ira, nec ignis, nec
poterit ferrum, nec edax abolerere vestustas. *Ovid*

Sta come torre ferma che non crolla Giammai la cima per
soffiar de 'venti. *Dante*

Ante victoriam ne canas triumpham. *Proverb*

Contents

Foreword

HIPPOCRATES SAID, "THE MAN WHO TREATS HIMSELF HAS A FOOL FOR A physician." This, perhaps, applies more to dancers than any other group of people—for nowhere are there more "fads" and hand-me-down remedies than in the "dancers' underground." In spite of all the progress that has been made in the accurate diagnosis and treatment of athletic and dance injuries, dancers continue to ask questions like, "Will my stress fracture heal faster if I eat bone meal?"; or one dancer will tell another what she did for her sore foot, suggesting that the other dancer obviously should do the same thing and her foot will heal—assuming blindly that it is the same problem, or that the first dancer's foot healed originally *because* of the treatment rather than *in spite of* the treatment.

Stuart Wright has written a valuable book to help the dancer make an accurate diagnosis of her problem and initiate a treatment plan based upon the diagnosis. It is especially useful in describing the minor injuries to the toes and forefoot.

I would like to reinforce several points made by the author:

1. If the treatment doesn't seem to be working—go see a doctor. There may be more going on than you suspect.
2. Don't use taping as a crutch. It's all right for a week or so while something heals, but it should not be used over a prolonged period of time to "cover up" an underlying weakness, for instance, that should be corrected by exercise—not by taping.

Good luck, stay healthy!

New York, 1983

WILLIAM G. HAMILTON, M.D.

9

Acknowledgments

MY GREATEST DEBT IS TO ALL THOSE DANCERS WHO ENCOURAGED ME TO gather together between the covers of this book the descriptions and methods presented. Their willingness to cooperate at the beginning of and throughout the progress of the making of *Dancer's Guide to Injuries of the Lower Extremity* has been invaluable. This book, then, is a tribute to them. I am especially indebted to Paige Whitley and Leslie Ancell for much assistance and many favors. I would also like to thank Katharine Turok, of Cornwall Books, for a sensitive reading of the manuscript and for many helpful suggestions, changes and alterations; this book is greatly improved for her part in it. Also special thanks go to Thomas Yoseloff for his encouragement.

For work in the preparation of the illustrative material contained in this book I would like to thank especially Joe Lechleider, of Impact Photographic Group, Winston-Salem, North Carolina, for his excellent photographs; the quality of his work is found on nearly every page. G. H. Raynor, of Raleigh, North Carolina, prepared the drawings under my supervision. Amy Pettyjohn and Holly Hoots, both of Winston-Salem, gave generously of their time in modeling for many of the photographs.

Others who have helped me in various ways, and whom I should like to thank, are Sal Aiello; Cathy Badia; Holly Barroway; Hallie Bellah; Shannon Bresnahan; Nancy Callahan; Melissa Clayton; Dr. George Core; Marina Eglevsky; Alesia Fowler; George P. Garrett; Patsy Gray; Dr. William G. Hamilton; Dr. John R. Iredale; Mark Land; Dr. Robert Lindgren; Dr. John Litcher; Dawn Loremann; Becky McClean; Dr. Charles McCreight; Michelle Mahanna; Ralph Miller; Carolyn Minor; Becky Myers; Joanne O'Brien; Michelle Paniagua; Marcia Plevin; Dr. J. Don Reeves; Dr. George D. Rovere; Maggie Sharp; Dr. Robert Suderburg; Dr. William Tribby; Polly Vogel; Laila Wiechmann; Steve Yates; and members of The Wednesday Club.

Publisher's Note

This book is intended as a guide to the most
common injuries suffered by dancers, and it is
the publisher's hope that dancers will find it useful in determining early or emergency treatment. However, it is not intended to supplant
your properly qualified physician. Throughout
the book the author cautions readers that only a
physician should prescribe required medication
or long-term treatment. Use this book with dis-
cretion and judgment of your own needs, and
know when professional care is called for. Happy
dancing!

Introduction

THIS BOOK IS FOR YOU, STUDENT AND PROFESSIONAL DANCERS, NOT FOR doctors. It is written in the simplest, nontechnical language. *Dancer's Guide to Injuries of the Lower Extremity* is based on my personal experiences with ballet and modern dance students at the North Carolina School of the Arts, in Winston-Salem, and with members of two professional companies, the North Carolina Dance Theater and Marcia Plevin Productions. Over a two-year period I met with these dancers regularly, listening to them discuss their injuries individually and in small groups, learning of their frustrations in finding adequate solutions to their problems, and helping them devise and modify for their use strapping and padding techniques that could help them.

Many of these dancers, like many of you, were reluctant to see a doctor because they thought they could "dance through" the problem or were afraid that the doctor would tell them to stay off the injured part for a period of time. (Dancers are all too aware of the physical consequences of a layoff, even of brief duration.) Or, worse yet, they were afraid to face the reality of what they perceived to be a serious injury, afraid to hear from the doctor that their dancing days were numbered, as if the problem, if ignored, would simply go away of its own accord. Things just don't work that way.

Dancers, like professional athletes, cannot, nor should not, ignore those daily aches and pains, no matter how insignificant they may think they are. A simple corn or callus can greatly upset a ballerina's sense of balance. The factors that have resulted in chronic shin-splints or lower leg pain, if left unattended, could eventually lead to a stress fracture or compartment syndrome. That stiffening of the big toe joint you thought you could just ignore or dance through but still has not improved just might end up permanently rigid. Or that

13

chronically painful, unstable knee that still hurts or feels weak because you insist on forcing turnout. It might just signal or hasten the end of your dance career.

The simple fact is that virtually all dance injuries result from faulty technique, whether complicated by anatomical anomalies or not. Let's face it: rare is the perfect body. Incorrect line and improper weight bearing are the principal predisposing factors to injury. *Technical correction is the best means to prevention and treatment.* The cause must be determined. But until you can begin such a regimen of rehabilitation, this book will greatly assist you in achieving symptomatic relief from many of the most common injuries that trouble you on a day-to-day basis.

The *Dancer's Guide to Injuries of the Lower Extremity* describes almost fifty common dance injuries, tells you how to recognize them, discusses what *you* can do about them, and advises you when to seek professional help. You will find in these pages many taping and padding techniques that will assist in stabilizing or protecting an injured part while it heals. Some of these techniques are rather simple and may be familiar to you already; others are not so simple and must be mastered by trial and error. Thus there is a good deal of "trouble shooting" throughout, helpful hints on what to expect if an injury is not healing properly or rapidly enough, what you experience if you apply a strapping too tightly or too loosely and so on.

Now, a word on anatomy and dance. Sadly enough, those dancers with whom I worked were particularly wanting in even the most basic elements of anatomy and kinesiology, to say nothing of biomechanics. *All* dancers, and their teachers, too, must realize the importance of a thorough study of the structures and movement of the body. The knowledge gained is absolutely essential, for it has been proven time and again, in survey after survey, that those dancers who have completed an intensive course of study in anatomy and kinesiology are not less injury prone but are, in fact, better dancers, better able to satisfy both physical and aesthetic demands of their art.

HOW TO USE THIS BOOK

Dancers are perhaps more aware of their bodies in general, and particularly, than any other group of performing artists. They know their limits and abilities and always are striving for regular improvement if not perfection. Because of the severe stresses and abnormal forces their bodies are subjected to, because rarely is any one of them blessed with the "perfect body," most dancers suffer to some degree *most* of the time, the extent of which is entirely individual, relative to the dancer's physical and psychological makeup. Because of their experientially gained knowledge, however, dancers usually have a fair idea of the type of injury they have sustained, whether it is a simple ankle sprain, a pulled muscle, Achilles tendinitis, a swollen bunion, or a painful corn or hammer toe.

Therefore I have divided this book into four regional categories: "Foot and Ankle," "Leg," "Knee," and "Thigh and Hips." There is, of course, constant overlapping of material in each category with the others because many, if not most, dance injuries proceed from the bottom up, starting with feet that sickle or roll in or out, weak ankles that are the product of frequent twists or turns, an inherent ligament laxity, abnormally high or low arches, and so on—all of which are constantly aggravated by improper technique. Nor can the knee be dealt with as an isolated unit: it is formed of thigh *and* leg bones, the cartilage that covers their surfaces, and the tendons that pass over them to cause movement. But, for the sake of simplicity of use, the regional approach of arrangement has been employed. You, the dancer, will know if the description you are reading applies exactly to what it is you observe, feel, or are experiencing. Moreover, your teachers should be glad to help you with the diagnostic process, using their own experience with injuries as a guide.

Most of the injuries described in this book cannot be easily confused with others. Only in certain general instances such as "arch pain" or "knee pain" may the exact identification require you to read several of the entries before the correct "diagnosis" is made. Dancers who have already used this book in its earlier, typed "handout" version have had few difficulties along these lines, even without the photographs and drawings contained here.

Once you have determined the nature and extent of your injury, you should carefully read the treatment section. Understand before beginning what will be required of you in terms of time and materials involved. Treatment paragraphs are accompanied by photographs and drawings that illustrate the techniques described, thereby reducing the chance for error.

Since the vast majority of dance injuries involve an inflammatory process, you will find that ice and aspirin are prescribed over and again. It is therefore important that we now discuss briefly each of these modalities so that you understand them better.

Aspirin as an anti-inflammatory agent yields extremely beneficial results in controlling tendinitis, bursitis, capsulitis, arthritis, and certain forms of joint inflammation. Its action is so effective, in fact, that some researchers have suggested that had aspirin been discovered recently instead of two centuries ago, it would be called a "wonder drug." But you must take *pure,* unbuffered aspirin to achieve the results. Aspirin substitutes such as Tylenol, (acetaminophen) or even buffered aspirin, simply do not do the job as well. These agents assist in pain relief but do not control inflammation. Specifically, you will have to take *at least* two five-grain (325 mg) aspirin every four hours for a period up to seventy-two hours to control an inflamed tendon or joint. You may take three or four aspirin every four hours if you can tolerate this amount, but forty grains per day—eight five-grain aspirin—constitute what is recognized as *minimum therapeutic dosage* for symptomatic relief. Finally, you must always take a *full glass of water (8 oz.)* with the aspirin to mitigate the irritating effects it can produce. WARNING: Prolonged use of aspirin is likely to cause severe gastrointestinal bleeding and may even produce permanent damage to the lining of the stomach. Aspirin should not be taken in conjunction with certain types of antibiotics (ask your doctor), any form of anticoagulant medication (blood thinners), other anti-inflammatory agents, or if you are taking corticosteroids or have a vitamin K deficiency or anemia. Some people are allergic to aspirin and must refrain from using it. Overdose is indicated by ringing in the ears, possible temporary loss of hearing, dizziness, headaches, or drowsiness.

Thus, while aspirin is heartily endorsed and recommended throughout this book and, indeed, could prove your best friend in dealing with a variety of inflammatory conditions, you should take precautions and be aware of its side effects and the symptoms of overdose. If any of these problems arises, discontinue use of aspirin and consult your physician immediately.

Ice as a therapeutic agent also goes far in reducing swelling and inflammation. There are several methods by which it can be applied, depending upon the location and size of the area under treatment. (1) Prepare an ice bath by adding a quantity of ice cubes or crushed ice to a basin of cold water. The basin should be deep enough to cover the injured part completely. (2) Fill a styrofoam cup with water and freeze it. When ready for application, tear away an inch or so of the cup from the solid mass. Hold it at the narrow end; and massage the area until the ice has melted away; then tear away more styrofoam, massaging as before. (3) Thoroughly soak a cotton hand-towel in water, fold it into a square or rectangle, depending upon the size and location of the area under treatment, and enclose it in a plastic bag, then freeze. The frozen towel may be laid over the area or held in place by an Ace or similar elastic bandage.

There are several elements of ice therapy that you should be aware of. For best results, the area should be iced until it is numb, which usually takes up to ten minutes, occasionally more. (Typically there is a period of inner warming that follows the numbing.) In the case of an ankle or knee joint, after the area has numbed, you should passively move the joint through its full range of motion for several minutes. (This does *not* mean doing a series of *arabesques* or *piqué* turns.) If time permits, this procedure, ice plus movement, should be repeated, followed by one more icing but without subsequent movement.

Elevation means keeping an injured part just above the level of the heart; it does not mean holding or propping it higher than your head. If you're elevating a knee or ankle, for instance, just lie down with the leg raised on several pillows.

There are many important remedial exercises that can be employed in stretching or strengthening an injured limb, but I have opted not to recommend or include many of them in this book. The reason is that each case is somewhat different, depending upon the dancer's age, level of ability, and so on; so we must depend upon a sensitive teacher or trainer to help you through this highly important stage of recovery and rehabilitation. Your teacher will know what is best for you at the barre and away from it. However, you must keep a few general rules in mind: do not begin to exercise a part if the injured area still hurts at rest; do not begin to exercise too quickly or at high levels of endurance, but build back slowly and gradually; if pain recurs during the initial phase of exercise—a *little* aching or fatigue can be expected—discontinue your program until it subsides.

The *Dancer's Guide to Injuries of the Lower Extremity* is designed to help you dancers help yourselves, to help you understand in simple terms the nature of the most common injuries that confront you, and more particularly, what you can do to care for these injuries. Since most dance injuries are not serious, there *is* much you can do in dealing with them. When simple methods of padding and strapping fail, however, you *must* consult a physician.

Here are some specific rules you should follow:

1. Your body talks, dancers. So listen. If it is screaming "PAIN," *consult a physician at once.*
2. If you have suffered the loss of movement or function of a part, or if you suspect that you have sustained an injury that involves ligaments or cartilage, *consult a physician at once.*

3. If the pain in an injured part persists unabated for a period up to two weeks, *consult a physician.*

While you may find the doctor's advice to "stop dancing" for a brief period something less than desirable, you should remember that it is *you alone* who must bear the consequences of negligence and inattentiveness if you do not heed his advice. It could mean an early end to your career if you fail to seek proper help when you need it.

So, dancers, use this book judiciously and wisely, in good health; let me hear from you if you have any questions, comments, or suggestions. *But see a physician if and when the occasion demands it.*

Dancer's Guide to Injuries of the Lower Extremity

1

Foot and Ankle

BLISTERS

BLISTERS ARE CERTAINLY COMMON ENOUGH AMONG DANCERS AND NOT surprisingly can be quite disabling if left unattended. Blisters are the result of the heat produced from friction and rubbing, especially in a warm, moist environment such as the inside of a pointe shoe. It is well to note that a blister usually begins as a "hot spot" (fair enough warning), a sore red spot on your heel, the top or side of your toe, wherever. You may in fact be able to prevent the blister from forming if you simply cover this "hot spot" with a Band-Aid or piece or cloth tape or oval of moleskin. Once the blister has formed, however, you must deal with it immediately, as it could lead to a bad infection, particularly if you have developed a blood blister involving deep tissues.

Treatment

If you have a clear blister, follow this procedure. Wash the area with warm, soapy water. After you have dried the area thoroughly, swab it with alcohol. Remember, the danger of infection is your greatest concern aside from the ordinary discomfort produced by the blister. Using a needle that you have sterilized over a flame or in alcohol, puncture the blister at three, four, or more points around its perimeter, close to where the blister joins healthy tissue. Gently press

21

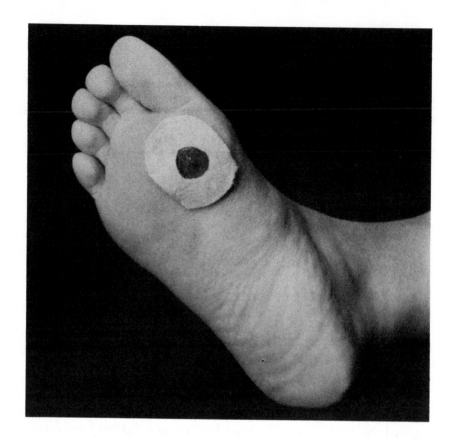

the top of the blister with a sterile gauze pad to evacuate the fluid within it. *Leave the skin intact and keep it protected.* You will reduce the chances of infection and the healing time in so doing. Next, cut an aperture pad from ⅛-inch felt, moleskin, or molefoam, depending on the area and size of the blister, and place it over the affected area so that the blister is within the aperture; a commercial bunion pad that has been beveled on all sides works quite well for large heel blisters. Fill the aperture with an antibiotic cream or ointment and cover with a piece of moleskin. The padding you have chosen should be thick enough to minimize the discomfort caused by the blister. Repeat the draining and padding procedure twice more over the next twenty-four hours. After several days the blister should no longer cause you any difficulty, and its "roof," the covering layer of skin, should have reattached to the base. *Note:* Recent studies have demonstrated that draining the blister three times during the first twenty-four hours and leaving the skin intact greatly reduces the healing time and minimizes the discomfort.

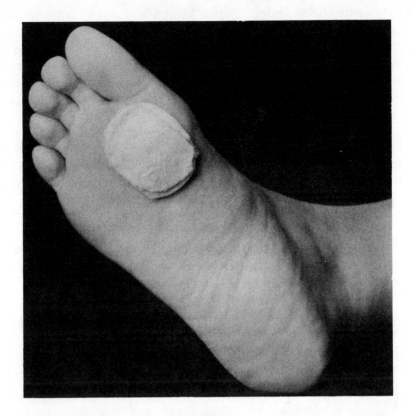

If you have developed a blood blister, not an uncommon occurrence among ballerinas in pointe shoes, you should consult a physician *immediately*. The risk of an infection is much too great to attempt self-treatment.

Preventing Blisters

If your toes are prone to blistering, lubricate them well with Vaseline and wrap them gently in wisps of lamb's wool or cotton. Remember, you can prevent blisters by covering the "hot spots" that precede them with moleskin. Powdering your feet with baby powder or any commercial antiseptic powder will also reduce your chances of forming a blister by reducing the amount of rubbing and friction against the skin.

HARD CORNS

A hard corn is a horny accumulation of skin most commonly found on the side or top of the fifth (little) toe, but also with some short pointe shoes. Indeed corns, like blisters, occur from the pressure and friction of poorly-fitted pointe shoes, and often from faulty technique. Pain results from pressure against the corn, which in turn presses against the underlying nerve endings within normal tissue. The corn itself does not contain blood vessels or nerves.

Treatment

Corns may be effectively eliminated if the source of friction is removed by proper padding. Several methods are possible. If you are intent on removing as much of the corn as you can before padding, this procedure is recommended.

1. Soak your foot in warm, soapy water for ten to twenty minutes.
2. After drying thoroughly massage into the corny mass any standard commercial vegetable oil, olive oil, or lanolin.
3. Next, with the coarse side of an emery board gently scrape away as much of the softened corn as you are able, then smooth it off with the fine side of the emery board.
4. Repeat on successive days, if necessary, until the corn has been reduced to the desired level or is flush with the skin. Routinely scrape the corn after every shower or bath to keep it under control.

If you insist on going after your corn with a blade, something that I cannot recommend entirely because of the danger of infection if you cut yourself in the process, you should follow this procedure.

1. Soften the corn in the manner described above. Obtain a professional corn chisel such as those illustrated or use a *single-edged* razor blade.
2. For your own safety remove only a thin layer with each succeeding cut. *Do not* try to remove the entire corn with a single cut. It is easiest to make a clean cut first time, avoiding a "sawing" action.
3. Try on your pointe shoes periodically to see if the desired level has been reached.
4. Once the corn is reduced, smooth it over with the fine side of an emery board and maintain it by scraping regularly after each shower or bath. Protect the area with an *unmedicated* corn pad.

Commercial corn removal medications are not recommended, nor are medicated corn pads. The danger of a burn from the medica-

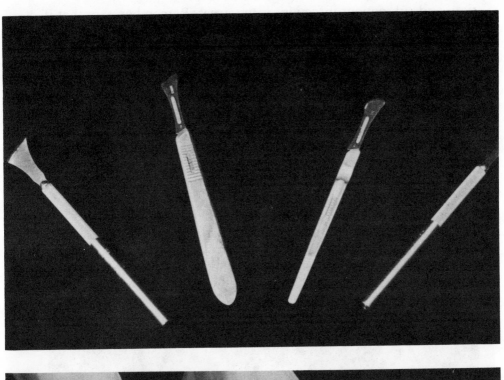

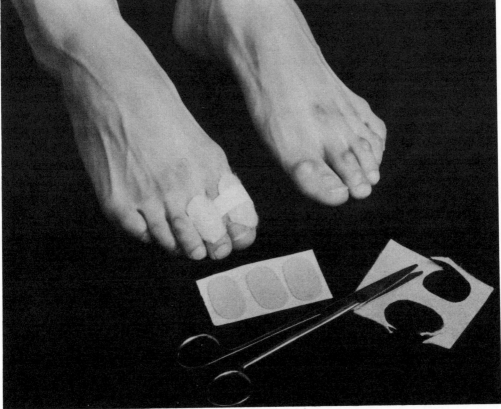

tion, and subsequent infection, is too great. Remember, too, that if you keep abnormal pressure off the toe—with moleskin or an unmedicated corn pad—even after the corn has begun to form, you can contain and even reduce it.

Small corns on the tops or sides of the toes can be dealt with by cutting out a layer of moleskin approximately the size of the toe and cutting a hole in its center just larger than the corn, so that the moleskin surrounds without touching the corn. Cut out a second piece as large as the first and cover. Secure with a strip of half-inch cloth tape. Or use a commercial unmedicated corn pad in this manner.

1. Prepare the skin by painting with benzoin or spraying with a pretape spray such as Tuf-Skin.
2. Place the corn pad directly behind the corn so that the wings of the "U" cradle the corn without touching it. Secure with half-inch cloth tape.

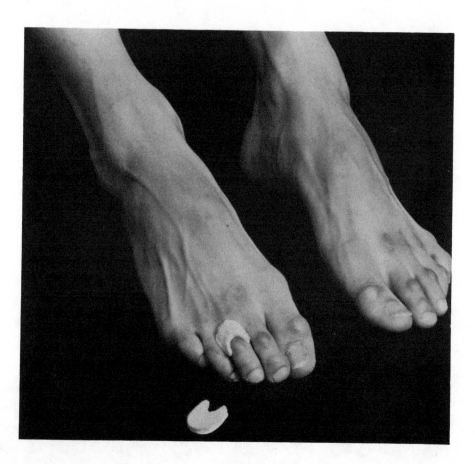

3. Or, prepare your own corn pad from sixteenth-inch or eighth-inch adhesive-backed felt, in the shape illustrated. Be certain to bevel all sides.

No matter how troublesome they are, all corns will eventually disappear if you keep them well padded. *Surgical removal is not recommended for dancers.*

SOFT CORNS

A soft corn is pathologically identical to a hard corn except that its location *between* the toes, not on the top or sides, results in rather a "mushy" soft appearance owing to the moist environment. Soft corns characteristically appear between the fourth and fifth toes, in the webbing, and present a blistery whitish-gray appearance. They are caused by tight pointe shoes that squeeze the metatarsal region, irritating the tissue that lies between the proximal phalanx of the fifth toe and head of the fourth metatarsal. Soft corns are a bit more serious than hard corns and also more difficult to treat because of their location. Always wear pointe shoes that are amply wide with a broad box.

Treatment

The object of treatment is to separate the opposing toes so as to eliminate the point where the bones have rubbed together to produce the corn. If you are successful at eliminating the source of pressure, and the area is allowed to dry thoroughly, the soft corn will disappear. Thus your first mode of treatment is simply to separate the opposing toes. For this purpose you may use a ball of lamb's wool or a commercially produced toe separator (see illustration). Keep the area dusted with a good astringent powder.

If keeping the toes separated for a period of time does not resolve the difficulty, you may want to gently remove the blister-like covering over the corn. But in doing so, remember that you are increasing the chances of an infection. As this blister is peeled away, you will probably notice a depression at its base. This depression has only a thin protective covering, but *leave it intact.* For class or performance, squirt a glob of Vaseline between the toes, then squeeze as much cotton or lamb's wool between them as you can, taking care that when pulling on your tights you do not dislodge it. As with hard corns, if you eliminate the pressure on the interdigital area, the soft corn will disappear.

27

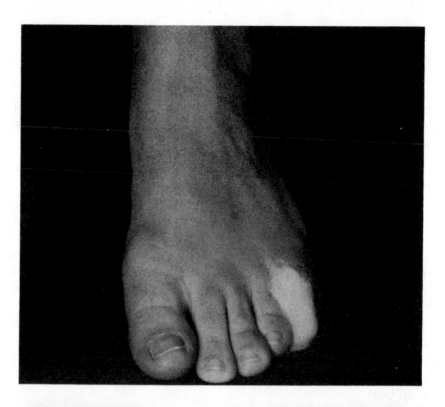

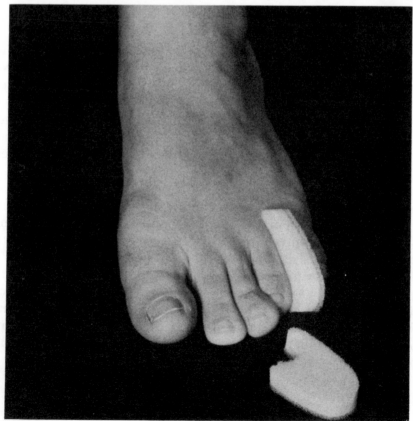

Surgical excision of soft corns is *not recommended,* but you should not hesitate to consult your physician if there are any signs of infection. Finally, *do not* under any circumstances use a medicated corn pad or liquid corn remover on a soft corn. The use of either will increase your chances of a bad burn and subsequent infection.

CALLUSES

Hard, thickened growths of dead skin beneath bony prominences on the sole of the foot or under the heel known as calluses are both a blessing and a curse. A certain amount of callus tissue is normal, even desirable for a dancer. But an excess of callus, resulting from poor posture, faulty weight bearing, especially if one of the metatarsal heads is more depressed than the others, or simply from improperly fitted pointe shoes, can lead to a very painful situation. Excessive abnormal pressure and friction complicate these predisposing factors. Some calluses, usually under the second metatarsal head, may develop within their mass a hard, cone-like nucleus, which makes the situation even more unbearable. Finally, because callus tissue is by nature inelastic, it moves as a mass and is therefore apt to tear or fissure (cracks appear within the surface of the callus), either of which could lead to a nasty infection. Dancers with flat or pro-

nated feet, or those with extremely high arches are especially prone to callus buildup.

Calluses, whether well defined or diffuse in appearance, become symptomatic when allowed to build up beyond a normal protective thickness. They become hot and extremely painful. If your heel tilts more to one side than the other then it is likely that a layer of callus will form on the tilted side. You may also have a thickened callus buildup on the side of your big toe due to an imbalance or faulty technique or both. Dancers who have bunions, with or without a short first metatarsal, usually have a thickened callus under the second metatarsal head because it must bear more than its normal share of body weight, owing to the unstable position of the first metatarsophalangeal joint. But regardless of these predisposing factors, any callus which is allowed to become too thick will give you more than a little trouble.

Treatment

The easiest way to deal with calluses is to prevent their building up to the point of pain. This is accomplished simply by filing away the top layers with an emery board or a homemade callus stick after

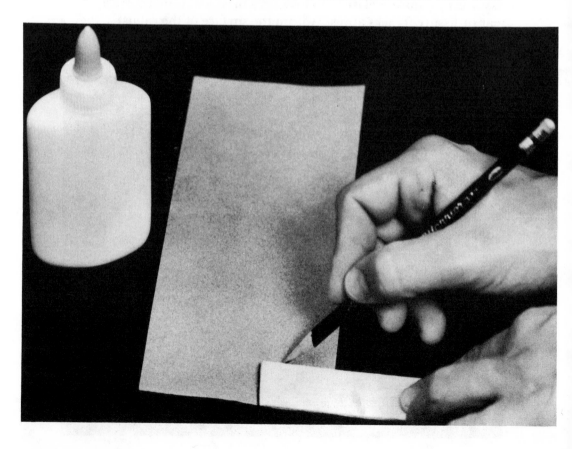

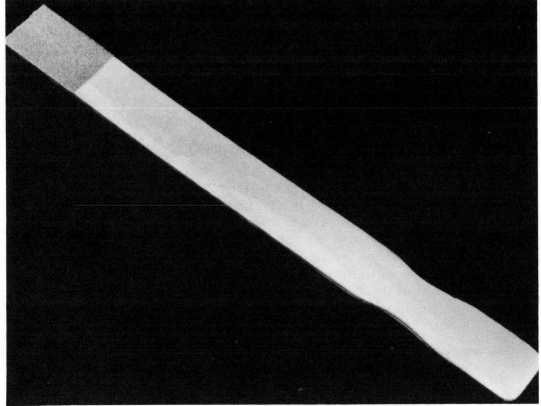

every shower or bath. To make your own callus file, take a wooden ruler or wooden paint stirrer and squirt some Elmer's glue on the end for a space of three or four inches. Place this end on a piece of fine sandpaper and outline. Once the glue has begun to harden cut away the excess sandpaper and place the file under several heavy books until completely hard. Repeat this procedure with a coarser piece of sandpaper on the other side of the stick. This sort of callus remover is easy to use and often a good deal more effective than those you can buy at the drugstore.

1. Soak your foot in warm, soapy water (two or three tablespoons of any mild liquid household detergent in a gallon of warm water) for ten to twenty minutes.
2. Dry your foot thoroughly with a towel, then rub into the callus any standard vegetable cooking oil or olive oil. This will further soften the callus.
3. File away the callus with the coarser side of an emery board or your callus stick, taking care not to remove too much callus at one time. File to a certain level then stop; try on your pointe shoes to see if you have taken away enough. Remove more callus if necessary, then smooth down with the fine side of the emery board or callus stick. *Note:* Be certain that the callus is perfectly flush with the skin all around and do not leave any raised or irregular areas around the perimeter of the callus.

It is a good idea to cover the area with a piece of moleskin or molefoam in which you have cut out a hole just larger than the callus. This will protect the skin until it begins to harden a bit.

If you have filed away too much callus, a painful condition in and of itself, you can achieve a degree of relief by padding it with eighth-inch adhesive backed felt. The wings of the pad should surround the painful areas without covering them.

To prevent callus buildup you may find that covering the affected area with a layer of moleskin is sufficient to sheer off excessive abnormal pressure. Do this before class or performance as necessary. *Note:* The biggest danger calluses present is when they are allowed to become too thick and break open. Because the tissue is inelastic, normal surrounding tissue may be torn as well. An infection might be the unfortunate result.

Calluses on the heel tend to be more troublesome during the winter months when your skin is dryer. Prepare the area by soaking in warm, soapy water as with any other callus. Rub in vegetable or olive oil. Since heel calluses tend to be a bit more shallow in places

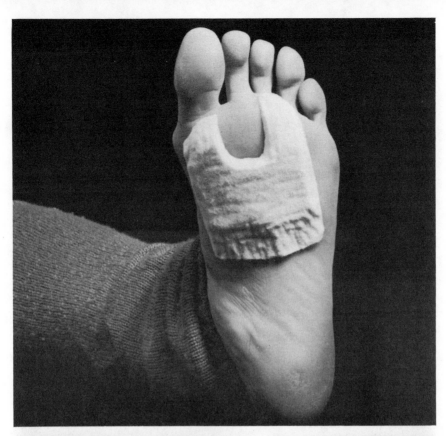

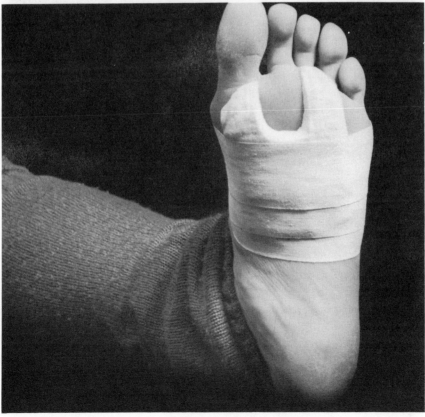

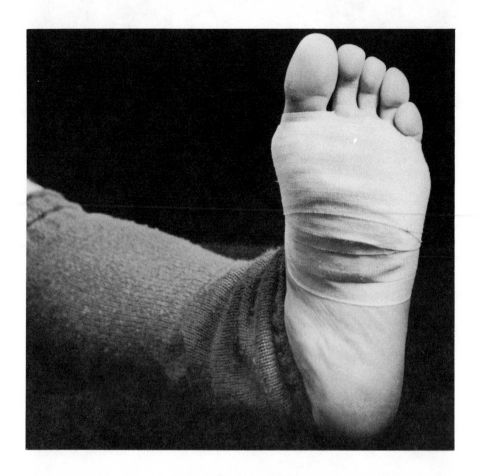

take care with your back and forth scraping motion that you do not damage healthy surrounding tissue. Once you have the heel callus under control use a protective layer of moleskin for class and performance as needed. Finally, the regular use of a good skin cream, which is massaged into the area, will keep the skin soft and pliable. Crisco, which is much less expensive than most hand creams, works very well for this purpose.

PLANTAR WARTS

A plantar wart is so called because of where it grows, on the sole of the foot or, technically, on the *plantar* surface of the foot. It is in most ways like any other wart except that it grows *in* instead of out because, for the most annoying of reasons, it chooses a weight-bearing surface such as under the heel, on the ball of the foot, or on the side of the big toe, in which to grow. Plantar warts are caused by a filterable virus which enters the tissue through a crack or cut. *Warts spread.* This is why, for instance, if you are a student living in a suite arrangement in a dormitory, sharing the same shower or tub with someone who has a plantar wart, you and your suite mates may get one as well. If this is the case, it is a good idea to put a full bottle or two of undiluted Chlorox in the tub or shower, letting it stand for eight hours or more to kill any viruses that may still be present. Chlorox is an excellent viricide and is readily available and inexpensive.

The mysterious thing about plantar warts is that while they may be quite uncomfortable, in and of themselves, even resistent to many forms of treatment (you may already have have them "cut out," frozen, burned, and so on), they will eventually *disappear.* This is a fact borne out by research and observation: a wart will eventually disappear entirely on its own, even though you may have had it for a year or longer. So, as a general rule, if you have had a plantar wart for an extended period of time and it has not gotten larger or started to spread, *leave it alone,* ignore it. If, however, the wart is causing you discomfort or is spreading, you may find that you can deal with it effectively on your own, with no interruption of class or performance.

Diagnosis

A plantar wart usually has a cauliflower-like appearance on its surface and may appear on your foot singly or in a group pattern of three, four, or many more (cases involving *hundreds* of warts on the same foot have been recorded). Often, in fact, you do not even realize that you have a plantar wart until you step on an irregular surface in a "funny way," causing a sidewise pressure against the wart which results in a sharp, shooting pain. If you are uncertain if what you have growing on your foot is a plantar wart, perform this simple diagnostic test:

> Press hard on the growth with the ball of your thumb. If only moderate pain or no pain at all is elicited, then squeeze the growth from the sides. A severe pain, sharp and shooting, indicates that you probably have a plantar wart. If, on the other hand, direct pressure hurts and squeezing does not, then you are probably dealing with an ennucleated callus.

Treatment

The object of treatment is to remove the wart slowly and pain-

PLANTAR WART OR CALLOUS?

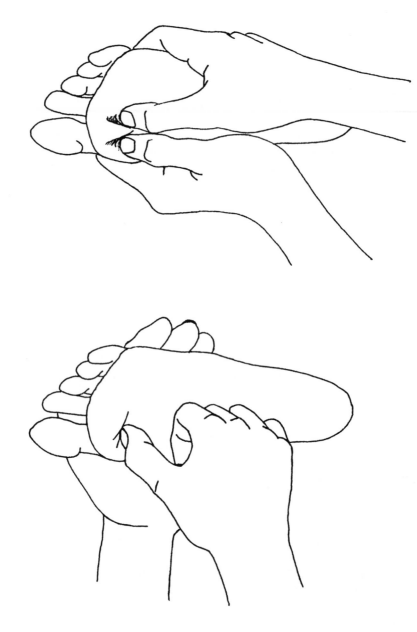

Pain produced from direct pressure usually indicates an ennucleated callous (hard, thick skin over a bony prominence).

Sharp, shooting pain from lateral pressure indicates a plantar wart.

lessly by such means that no painful scar is left behind. The simplest and most effective method is the application of 40 percent salicylic acid plaster (obtainable from your pharmacist without prescription) directly to the wart, with daily removal of the cauterized tissue. In general, standard commercial wart removers are not so effective in dealing with plantar warts. *Under no circumstances is surgical excision of the wart recommended;* the likelihood of postoperative scar formation or recurrence of the wart itself are much too great. *Note:* In treating a group of warts, never cover the entire area with the acid plaster. Deal only with the largest wart or two in the group. For some mysterious reason the smaller warts often disappear if the large "mother" wart is destroyed. Such a pattern of spreading warts may, however, dictate your seeing a dermatologist for treatment. He is likely to choose a more dramatic method, electrocautery or freezing, for instance. However, both methods are quite effective but will probably cause you to lose some time from class while the area heals.

For a single wart, this method of removal is recommended:

1. Using a cotton swab or Q-tip, coat the skin around the wart with

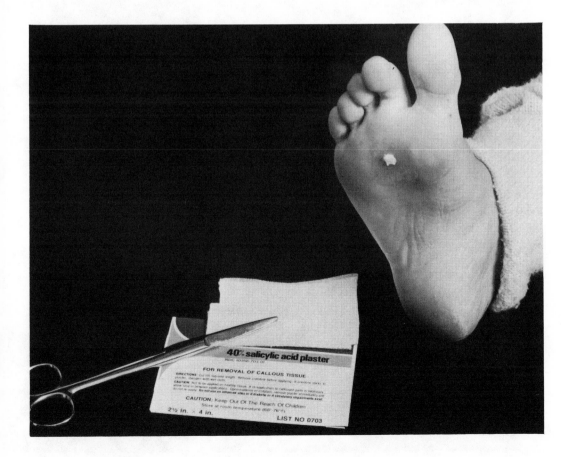

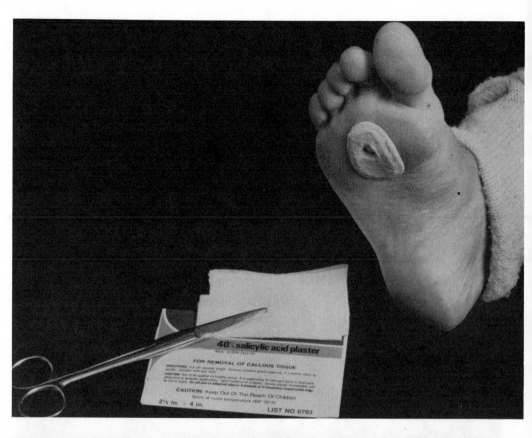

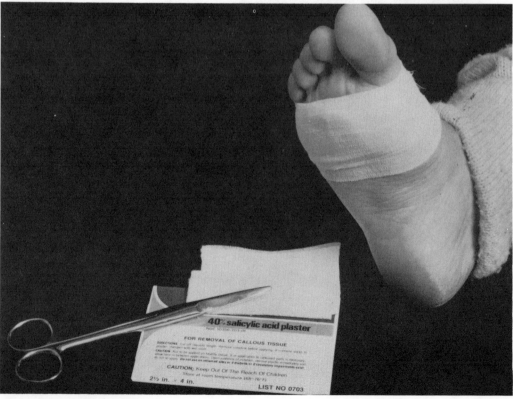

several layers of flexible collodion (available from your pharmacist) or clear nail polish. This will protect the tissue immediately surrounding the wart. Remember, you must not cover the wart itself with collodion, or the acid will not penetrate its surface.

2. Cut out a piece of adhesive-backed salicylic acid plaster the size of the wart, or just slightly smaller, and attach it to the surface of the wart.

3. Bevel the sides of an *unmedicated* corn or bunion pad, or cut your own from eighth-inch felt or moleskin, cutting a hole in the center, and place it over the wart. The hole in the pad should surround the wart without coming in contact with it.

4. Cover the aperture (or hole) in the pad with a piece of plastic adhesive tape or moleskin and secure in place with a piece of cloth tape.

It is necessary that you keep the area absolutely dry for *at least* twelve hours. You must not decrease the strength of the acid by diluting it with water. At the end of twenty-four hours remove the dressing. The wart and perhaps some of the tissue immediately surrounding it will have a white, puffy appearance from the cauterizing effect of the acid. This surface may now be carefully scraped or cut away with a single-edged razor blade or scalpel, or snipped away with a pair of small, sharp scissors or tissue nippers. *Remove only the white, cauterized tissue,* taking care not to nick or cut yourself. Not only is there the danger of infection, but you will have to skip the next treatment until the area heals over.

After the first treatment or two you will notice within the body of the warty tissue groups of black or brownish-black dots. These are cauterized capillary endings and should be expected; warts have a rather large blood supply. Follow this procedure of removing bits of the wart and reapplying the acid until the wart is completely destroyed. *Note:* Most plantar warts are clearly defined or circumscribed, so it is easy for you to differentiate between warty and pink, healthy tissue. If you have removed the wart patiently and carefully, layer by layer, you will probably discover at its base a white stalk or string-like cord, which is the vascular bundle of the wart. You should apply one more piece of acid plaster to obliterate it and any remaining warty tissue around it.

The pit or crater that remains after the wart has been removed will heal quickly and naturally, from the inside out. For comfort you may want to keep the area padded with moleskin for another week or so, or as long as is necessary. One final note: if at any time during the treatment the area becomes painful, skip your treatment for a day or so. The total length of time involved could last from one week to three or more. Be patient, however, and your efforts will be rewarded.

THICKENED TOENAILS

A thickened toenail, often grayish black or brown in color, is the result of constant jamming in your pointe shoe. The extra thickness of nail that forms in response to the pressure creates additional pressure against the nail bed. These thickened nails can be quite painful, but you can deal with them effectively if they have not built up too thickly. *Note:* A thick nail that takes on a yellowish brown color and exhibits an accumulation of spongy debris beneath it may indicate a fungal infection. If you suspect such a condition, do not fail to consult your doctor or a dermatologist immediately; this sort of thing is beyond your ability to treat and may become worse by spreading to other toes.

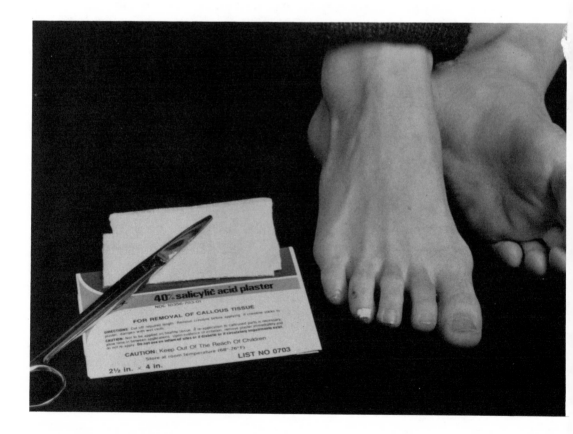

Clean the toe thoroughly with soap and warm water, soaking for fifteen to twenty minutes. With a probe or nail file clear out as much of the matter beneath the corners and sides of the nail as you can. (This procedure may be mildly uncomfortable.) Next, cut a piece of 40 percent salicylic acid plaster (obtainable from your pharmacist) just slightly smaller than the toenail and attach to its surface. Cover with a piece of adhesive tape. Now comes the difficult part: you must keep the toe completely dry for forty-eight hours. After this period remove the tape and residue of acid plaster and scrape away the flaky material with an emery board or old toothbrush. Clean the area with warm, soapy water, dry, and, if needed, reapply the salicylic acid plaster for another twenty-four hours. Sometimes two or three applications are necessary to reduce the thickened nail, so do not become discouraged if you have to repeat the treatment. If any discomfort is experienced, skip several days before reapplying. You may find that covering the toe with a layer of foam tubing provides a degree of relief during the first week or so after you have reduced the thickness of the nail.

Some dancers deal with the problem of thickened nails with a

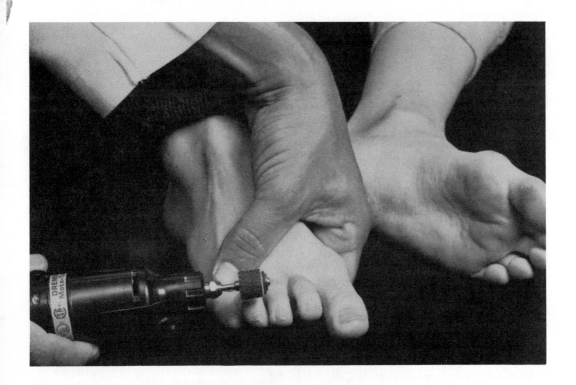

Dremel woodworking drill, using the sanding drum attachment. If you have access to such a drill and wish to try this technique, you must remember that you cannot hold the sanding drum against the nail for more than a fraction of a second because of the friction and heat generated. A series of quick repeated swipes over the nail surface works best. You will be surprised how effective this drill can be, and how much nail you are able to remove painlessly. Take care not to sand off too much. Try on your pointe shoes periodically to see if the proper thickness has been attained.

BRUISED TOENAILS

Constant, unrelenting pressure from pointe shoes that are too short or narrow for your feet may cause the blood vessels beneath the toenails, especially of the great toe, to rupture. Since there is no means by which this blood may escape, a clot or hematoma forms beneath the nail. The increased pressure which results is extremely painful and debilitating. If you can treat the nail within twenty-four to forty-eight hours after the blood has entered the area between the toenail and nail bed, there is a good chance you can save the nail. If, however, you do not treat the condition early enough, you may lose the nail over the next two to four weeks. *Note:* If the toenail begins to detach itself from the toe you should secure it in place with half-inch cloth adhesive tape. This will protect the sensitive underlying tissue from further injury. If you lose the nail, it will take up to six months for a new one to grow in. This new toenail may grow in somewhat thickened, especially if you have traumatized the nail by dropping something on it. Nevertheless, it is likely that a healthy nail will replace the thickened one.

Treatment

To relieve the pressure that results from accumulated blood beneath the nail you will first have to arouse yourself to a degree of courage. Remember, however, that the thought of what you must do is really much worse than the actual performance of the task.

Heat a paper clip red-hot over a live flame (you may have to hold it in a hemostat, if you have one, or a pair of fine pliers) and quickly, before the paper clip cools down, press against the nail surface. Hold it there until it melts through. Several reheatings may be required before you get through. If you are very careful, there should be little or no discomfort whatsoever, only relief as the trapped blood escapes—often with a dramatic spurt! If on the other hand a

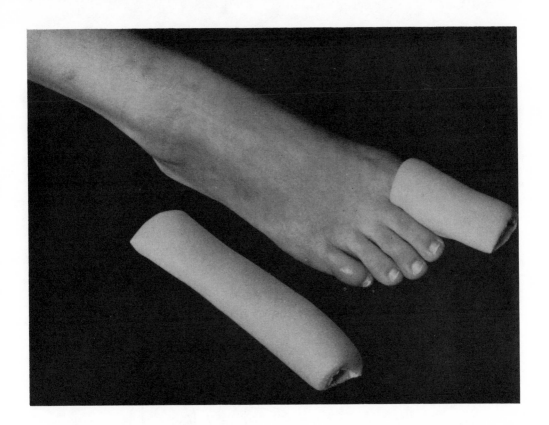

clot has already formed, you may have to press gently on the sides of the nail to decompress the area entirely. For the next seventy-two hours you should soak your foot three times daily in warm water with Epsom salts or Domeboro tablets (two tablespoons per gallon of water). Paint the nail with benzoin or Merthiolate and keep it covered with a Band-Aid or cloth adhesive tape. You can obtain additional relief from the pressure of shoes by wearing a foam tube covering over the toe. *Note:* If you ice the bruised nail immediately after the injury and continue to ice it periodically thereafter, you may be able to prevent the painful accumulation of blood beneath it. If the nail begins to come off, which it probably will, keep it attached as long as possible, or until the new nail begins to grow through, in order to protect the sensitive tissue beneath.

INGROWN TOENAILS

An ingrown toenail occurs when the side of the toenail, usually the *inside* of the great toenail, burrows into the surrounding skin. It may be the result of several complicating factors: (1) improper cutting of the toenails; (2) the pressure of pointe shoes that are too tight; or (3) nails that have thickened in response to repeated pointe work. Initially the nail groove becomes red and sensitive; then there is swelling along the edge; and finally an inflammatory process ensues as the healthy tissue rejects the nail edge or as it punctures the surrounding tissue allowing bacteria to enter.

Diagnosis

Severe, sharp pain is experienced at and around the point where the ingrown nail has broken the skin. There is redness and swelling in response to the presence of a foreign body, the nail fragment, which has lodged in the skin. *Note:* If there is any sign of pus or deep infection DO NOT try to handle this problem yourself. Go see a doctor immediately.

Treatment

To remove a simple ingrown toenail follow this procedure. Soak your foot in a gallon of warm, soapy water for at least twenty min-

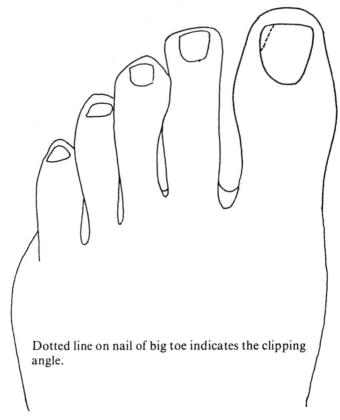

Dotted line on nail of big toe indicates the clipping angle.

utes. This cleans the area and softens the nail. With a good pair of sharp toenail clippers cut through the nail at an angle of approximately thirty to forty-five degrees. This is accomplished by inserting the clippers under the nail and exerting an even, forward motion toward the side of the nail, then CLIP. Make no mistake about it: no matter how careful you are, this will probably hurt like hell. So try to make a clean cut first time, all the way through the nail. If you leave nail fragments behind, there is a good chance the problem will recur. The severed nail fragment can be gently removed with a forceps or tweezers, or, if you are careful, with a simple twisting action of the nail clippers. Next, cleanse the area with hydrogen peroxide.

This done, fill the nail groove with an antiseptic ointment and cover the end of the toe with a Band-Aid or cloth adhesive tape. A tubular foam shield will protect the toe from additional pressure from your street shoes. You will probably find that wooden clogs are more comfortable to wear because of the greater width across the toes.

Now that the offending portion of the nail has been removed, you *must* follow up in this manner for the next week or so. Soak your foot for at least fifteen to twenty minutes, three times daily, in warm water (one gallon with two tablespoons of Epsom salts or two Domeboro tablets). Dry thoroughly and paint the affected area with benzoin or Merthiolate to assist in drying and hardening it. Con-

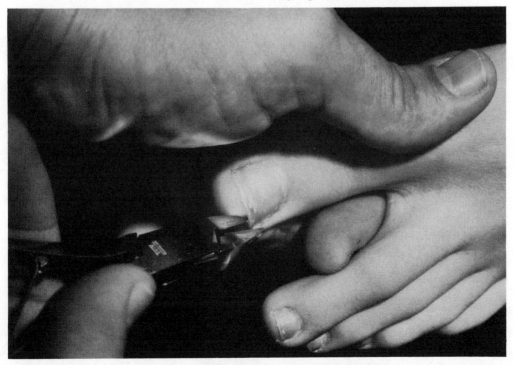

tinue with your antibiotic ointment, Band-Aid, and tubular covering (as needed) until the nail has grown out sufficiently to insert a wisp of cotton or lamb's wool under it. This will insure that the nail will continue to grow up and out, away from the nail groove. Use tubular foam in your pointe shoes to reduce the pressure on the side of your toe.

Here are some pointers for you to remember. Never trim your nails too short or allow them to grow too long. They should be cut straight across and rounded very slightly on the ends, *if at all.* A nail that is too long is better than one that is too short: a healthy, longish nail will not grow in (unless it develops a spicule, or needle-shaped body, on the side). Dancers know that nails which are too short will cause problems in pointe shoes until toe callus is built up; use a lamb's wool covering as a buffer, if necessary. Some dancers say that cutting a V-shaped wedge out of the center of the nail will relieve the pressure of an ingrown nail; others say it will not. Enough dancers have told me of their success with this technique to justify a reserved recommendation. However, after you have cut out the V, it is still a good idea to pack a wisp of cotton or lamb's wool under the corner of the nail plate.

But most important, remember that there is no substitute for a good pair of nail clippers. These are used not just in emergency situations such as an ingrown nail but for routine care and trimming as well. You may have to spend up to twenty dollars, but your invest-

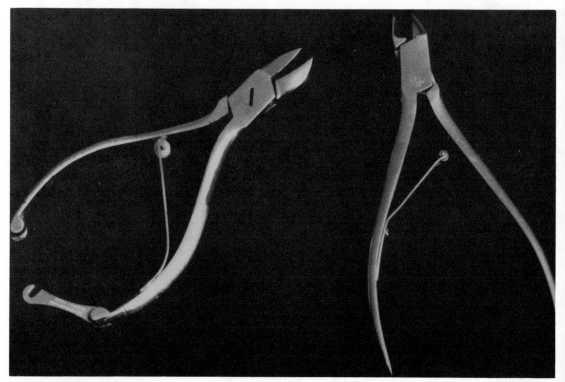

ment is sound and longterm. *Note:* Sometimes a chronic ingrown nail condition is accompanied by the formation of hard callus tissue in the nail groove. If left unattended this callus will become hard and flaky, eventually causing a degree of discomfort in and of itself. You can deal with this annoying condition by saturating the nail and nail groove with warm olive oil to soften it. Wipe away the excess oil with a cotton ball or Q-tip. Next, gently raise the nail edge with a forceps or tweezers and scrape away the callus formation with a nail file or emery board you have sharpened to a point for the purpose. This procedure is relatively painless and will spare you a great deal of discomfort later on.

HAMMER TOES

Under ideal circumstances, a ballerina's first and second toes are the same length; but this is rarely the case. In fact, you probably know dancers who dance on the "knuckles" of their second toes. Hammer toes occur when a short shoe and a long toe collide. This toe, usually the second, buckles to accomodate itself to the pointe shoe as well as to the length of the great toe. The extensor tendon on top of the toe eventually becomes shorter owing to this contracted position. In time the joint becomes more or less locked. This condition in and of itself is not altogether undesirable, but corns fre-

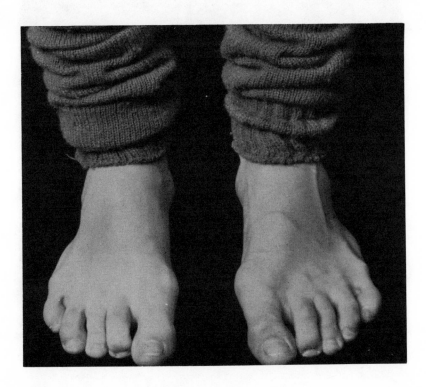

quently form at the point where the joint buckles or at the tip of the toe or sometimes at both places. The corn in fact is what usually causes the discomfort that develops from a hammer toe.

Treatment

The corn that forms on top of the toe should be regarded and treated as any other corn (see "Hard Corns"), and for reasons of personal safety, filing or scraping is recommended over trimming with a blade. An aperture pad or U-shaped corn pad works quite well in protecting the toe from further rubbing.

1. Paint the toe with benzoin or spray with pretape spray such as Tuf-Skin.
2. Apply a commercial U-shaped felt corn pad *behind,* not over or in front of the corn. Strap into place with a strip or two of half-inch cloth adhesive tape.
3. Or, place a foam aperture pad *over* the corn and strap into place.

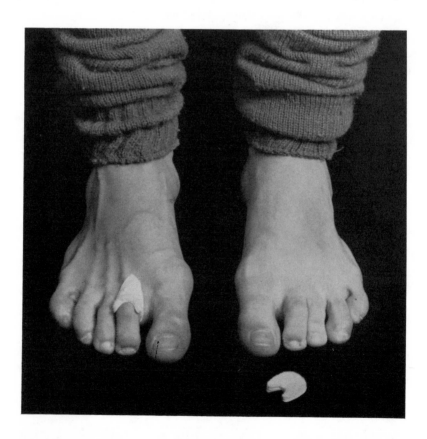

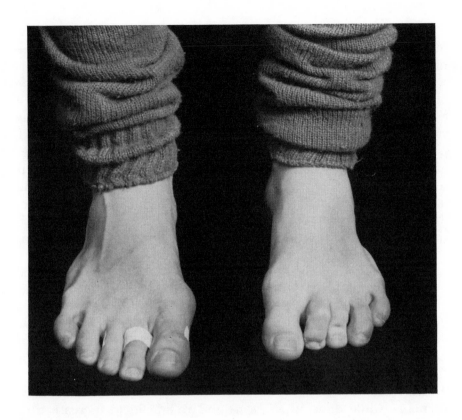

For rehearsal or performances you may also want to strap the toe in a straightened position. In the illustration that accompanies this description it is the second toe that is hammered and strapped to its neighbors, the great and third toes.

1. Take a strip of half-inch cloth adhesive tape and measure with the non-sticky side from the outer side of the third toe, under it, and over the hammered second toe, to the corresponding outer side of the big toe.
2. Cut this length of tape and apply, sticky side in.

Finally, you must understand that once a hammer toe has formed it is *correctable* only by surgery. Surgery, however, while technically simple enough to perform, is not recommended. Most orthopedists who treat dancers generally agree that it is actually better for you to continue to strap, scrape, and pad as needed.

The terms hallux valgus and bunion are often used synonymously, even by many health professionals. Technically, however, hallux valgus is a dislocation, as it were, of the first metatarsophalangeal joint in which the first metatarsal deviates toward the other foot, the result of which is a knob-like eminence on the side of the foot that is subject to abnormal stresses and pressure. Hallux valgus is more common among females than males, and there appears to be a hereditary predisposition to the condition. Does either of your parents or your grandparents have the condition? Does your second toe appear longer than the first toe? You may have a congenitally short first metatarsal that often occurs with hallux valgus. Does the ball of your foot tend to be rather flexible or pliable? Does it spread out a bit, or splay, with weight-bearing? Such flexibility is commonly observed in persons with hallux valgus.

A *bunion* is an inflamed bursal sac that lies between the angulated first toe joint and the skin and is secondary to the deformity. This bursal sac attempts to decrease friction against the joint by forming a protective fluid-filled buffer. Increased pressure and friction cause this sac to distend with fluid, however, thereby increasing the size of the joint. In fact, you have probably already noticed that when your "bunion" is most painful, it is red and swollen. This is the result of the inflamed bursa.

Finally, while dancing *en pointe* and rolling in to increase turn turnout during a *grand plié* may cause a mild degree of hallux valgus by stretching the ligaments on the inside of the foot, those dancers who have the most difficulty with this condition will most likely tell you that they have always had the "bunion" to some degree, but until they began to dance, it did not give them any appreciable degree of discomfort.

Because the angulated joint protrudes, it is subject to excessive and abnormal stress and friction, especially from tight-fitting pointe shoes. The skin appears hot and red as the joint swells. You feel a sharp or aching sensation within and around the joint, which often persists even after you have removed your pointe shoes. Indeed, any type of footwear that presses against the area is generally found to be unacceptable.

Treatment

The object both of prevention and treatment is essentially the same, to protect the joint in such a way that abnormal shearing and

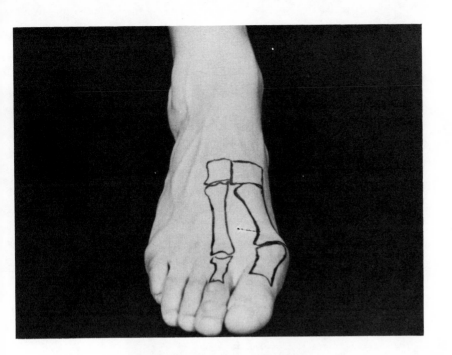

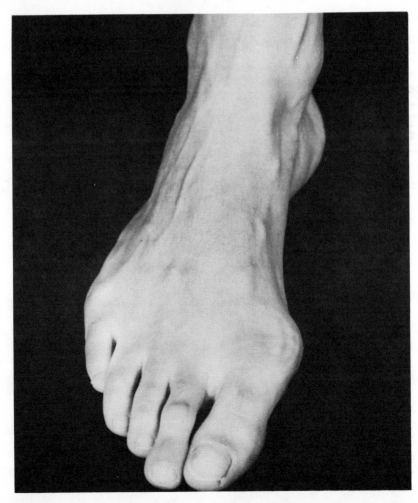

HALLUX VALGUS AND BUNION

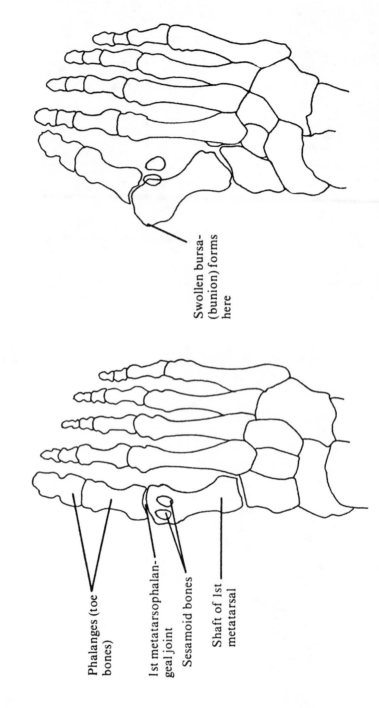

Phalanges (toe bones)

1st metatarsophalan- geal joint

Sesamoid bones

Shaft of 1st metatarsal

Normal position of 1st metatarsal, distal phalanx, and sesamoid bones.

Swollen bursa- (bunion) forms here

Dislocated position of 1st metatarsophalangeal joint in hallux valgus deformity. Note the position of the inner sesamoid.

rubbing is prevented, or at the very least, minimized. However, if the joint is inflamed, ice it for ten to fifteen minutes after class; this will help reduce the swelling. You should also take aspirin, three or four every four hours for the first three days, and two every four hours thereafter, as needed. Also, for rehearsals or class, you should cut wedges out of the sides and back of your pointe shoes and replace them with elastic or moleskin. Additional pressure may be removed from the joint if you cut several slits through the inside of the box of your pointe shoes.

Removable bunion pads may be used on a day to day basis to protect the joint. Also, many dancers have found that a large or extra large foam toe separator realigns the joint sufficiently to re-move a degree of pressure from the bunion for long-term relief. *Note:* Do not tape the first toe to the second with a separator between them; this puts an excessive abnormal strain on the already unstable first toe joint. All you need to do, simply, is insert the separator between the toes. It will stay in place. If you do not have a toe separator, or cannot obtain one quickly enough, you can insert a large wad of lamb's wool between the tips of the first and second toes.

Some dancers have found that the nightly application of an occlu-sive dressing containing 10 percent Ichthyol ointment helps reduce the inflammation. This is accomplished, simply, by saturating a

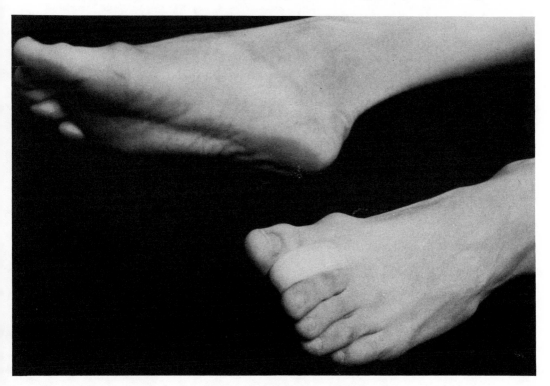

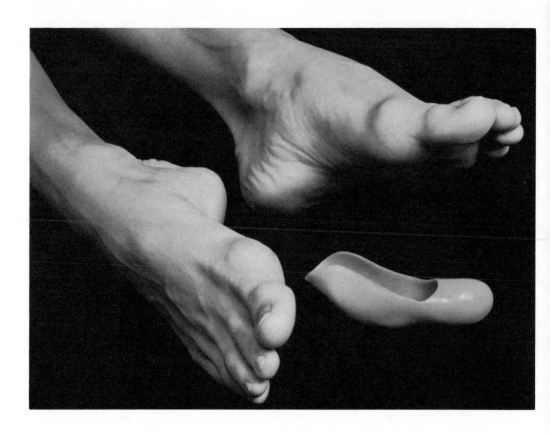

gauze pad in the solution (which is readily obtainable from a pharmacist) and placing it over the affected joint at night before you go to bed. The front of the foot should be carefully wrapped in Saran wrap which is secured with tape. The dressing is removed in the morning when you get up.

You may also want to obtain a premolded latex bunion shield which, for some dancers, provides the degree of relief they need.

Most effective of all, however, is felt padding fitted directly around the joint, either with one or two precut bunion pads, or custom-cut from one-eighth- or three-eighths-inch felt. This pad will take the pressure off the joint by filling the contour of the inside border of the foot, in front of and behind the angulated joint, in such a way that it in effect no longer protrudes. Forces are thereby more efficiently sheared from it, and friction is greatly reduced.

METHOD 1

1. Prepare the skin by painting with benzoin or spraying with a pretape spray such as Tuf-Skin.

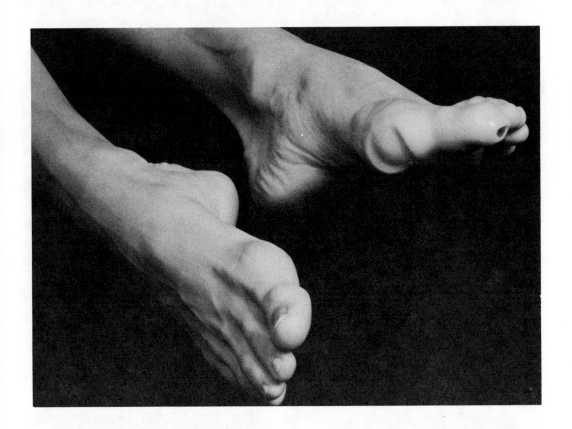

2. Take one or two precut bunion pads, depending upon the size of the joint, and bevel on all sides, slightly more in front than back. If you are using two bunion pads, stick them together first, before beveling.
3. Attach the pad to the skin in such a way that it completely surrounds the joint but does not come in contact with it. You may need to increase the size of the aperture (hole) slightly; just insert your index fingers and pull until the right shape has been achieved.
4. Strap into place with one-eighth or three-eighths-inch cloth tape.

METHOD 2

1. Prepare the skin by painting with benzoin or spraying with a pretape spray such as Tuf-Skin.
2. Cut an elongated rectangle from one-eighth- or three-eighths-inch adhesive-backed felt. Round the edges front and back.
3. Bevel the pad on all sides, again, taking more from the front than the back.

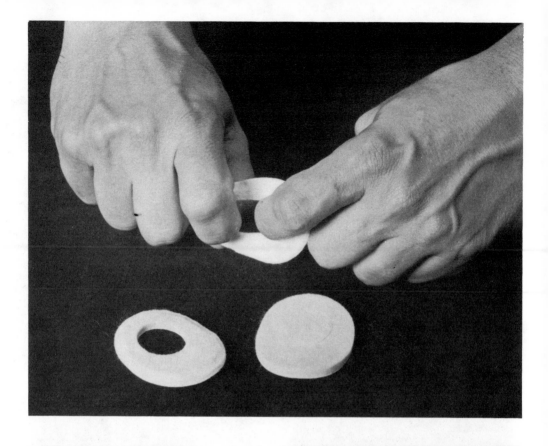

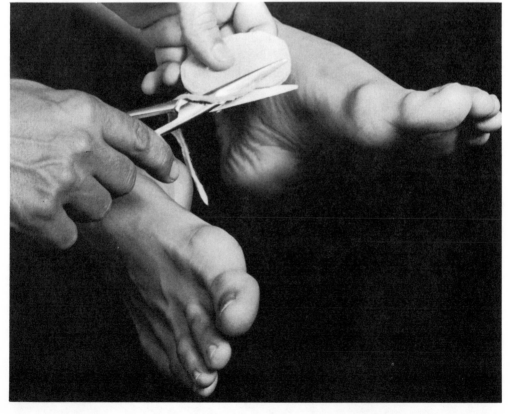

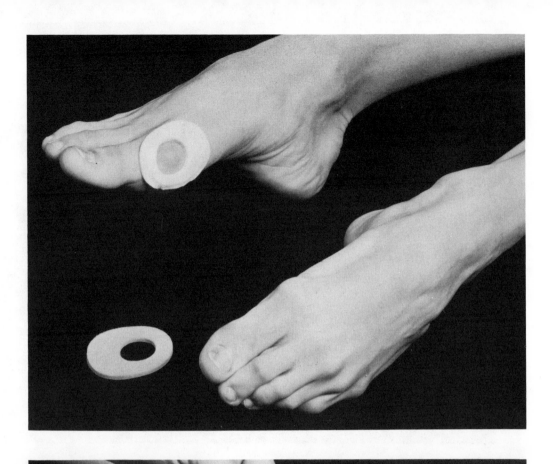

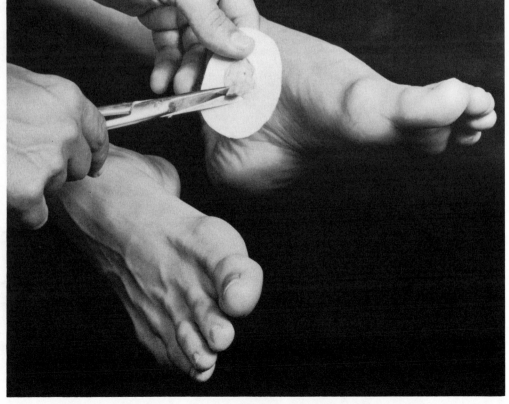

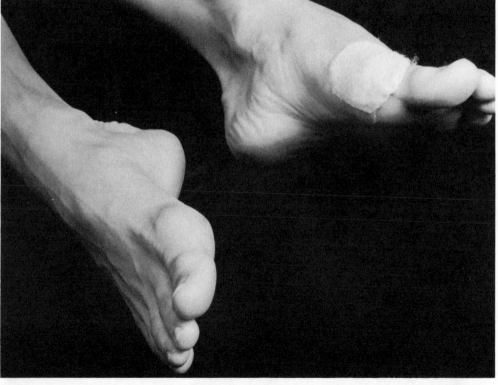

4. Cut a pocket in the pad just larger than the distended joint. This pocket should not go quite through, so take care when cutting it. Using your thumb or index finger push the pocket out and to the sides to make the felt roof just a bit more pliable.
5. Place your pad in position around the joint and secure with strips of 1 or 1½-inch cloth tape.

One final note on padding. Frequently the inner sesamoid bone under the great toe joint becomes inflamed because of its somewhat exposed location. You may need to pad it as well; but realize that the total bulk of both pads may not easily fit into your pointe shoe. You might find, however, that this is your only temporary recourse. Both pads should be in position before you apply your tape strips.

Bunion padding, like any other, may be left in place for two or three days. Still, it is a good idea to remove it during periods of relative inactivity, over the weekend, for example, if you are a student, in order to give the foot a chance to "breathe" and to reduce the chances of local skin irritation. Remember, too, this sort of padding works very well in keeping the condition from becoming worse, but it might take three to five weeks or more before all of the discomfort of a severely inflamed bunion to disappear, depending, of course, on the age of the dancer, the degree of severity of the deformity, and the duration of symptoms.

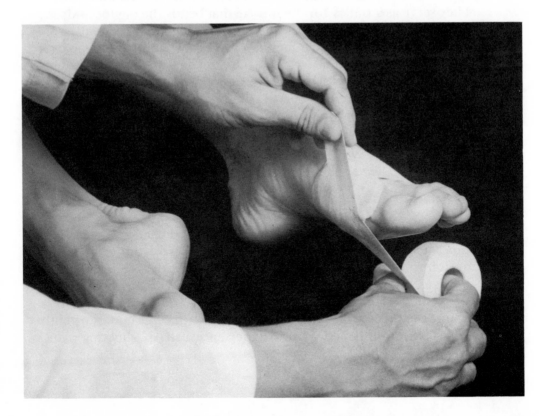

Surgery

While surgical correction of a hallux valgus may in fact produce excellent cosmetic results—a straight toe—the dancer usually ends up with a degree of limited motion in the affected joint. Also, those dancers who have undergone surgical correction of hallux valgus early in their career have found that *demi-pointe* is permanently limited. Therefore surgery is *not* recommended to the student or professional during the course of his or her career. Be wary of any doctor who suggests even the "simplest" bunion procedures. Consult an orthopedist who understands and treats dancers. Remember, many dancers who have had the enlarged joint "shaved" down or the bursal sac removed have not benefited at all from the inconvenience and discomfort; and some, in fact, have had to endure chronic pain as the unfortunate result.

SESAMOIDITIS

Notice in the drawings that accompany this section the two pea-shaped bones that lie within the belly of the flexor hallucis brevis muscle beneath the first metatarsal head. These are sesamoid bones. They serve as a pulley for the muscle that bends the big toe and also function as the weight-bearing surfaces of the first metatarsophalangeal joint. Protruding as they do beneath the metatarsal head, they are easily injured. If you have a bunion, or hallux valgus deformity, it is likely that the innermost of the two sesamoids lies within the interspace between the first and second metatarsal heads and is even more prone to injury. Sesamoiditis occurs more commonly in dancers with thin bony feet that have little protective padding across the ball. Leaps and jumps on hard, uneven surfaces hasten the onset of this painful condition.

Diagnosis

When the sesamoids are inflamed, you find that *demi-pointe* becomes extremely difficult owing to severe pain under the first metatarsal head. This pain is also present to a degree in everyday footwear, but pointe shoes make it even worse. Ultimately there will be swelling around the joint. To confirm your suspicions press against the metatarsal head from below. If either sesamoids or both are bruised or inflamed you will experience a sharp, shooting pain.

SOLE OF RIGHT FOOT SHOWING THE SESAMOID BONES
UNDER BIG TOE JOINT

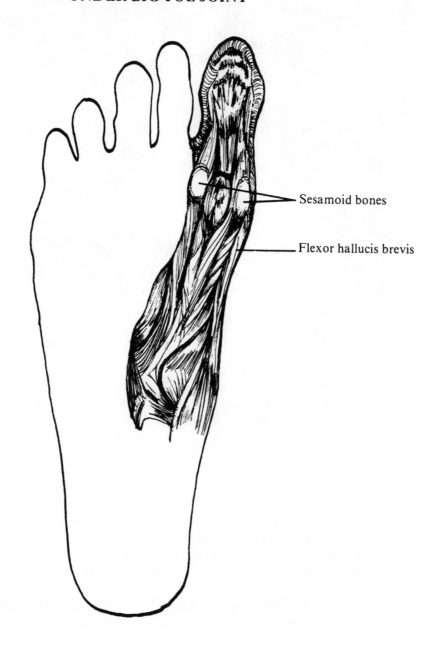

Sesamoid bones

Flexor hallucis brevis

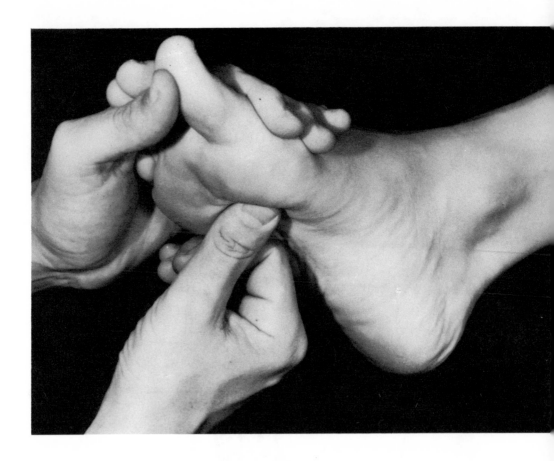

Treatment

Early on you should ice the foot for fifteen to twenty minutes three times daily. Take aspirin, three or four every four hours for three days, two every four hours thereafter as needed. Padding the foot in this manner will also afford a degree of relief.

1. Prepare the skin by painting with benzoin or spraying with pre-tape such as Tuf-Skin.
2. Cut out and bevel an adhesive-backed felt pad, one-quarter- or three-eighths-inch, that extends from the inner border of the foot across it, coming just behind the inner metatarsal heads, and extending back to a point that approximates the midfoot.
3. Strap into place with 1- or 1½-inch cloth adhesive tape.

You may find that you will have to keep the sesamoids padded for a week or more before the symptoms subside significantly, and some of the pain may persist for a month or more. It is a good idea to put as much extra sponge padding in your shoes as you are able, and a thin layer in your pointe shoes as well. Wooden clogs with inflexible soles are good for everyday wear. If the symptoms have not subsided significantly within ten days to two weeks you should consult an orthopedist who can tell you if one of the sesamoids is fractured. If this is the case you will probably have to wear for a cast for a brief period.

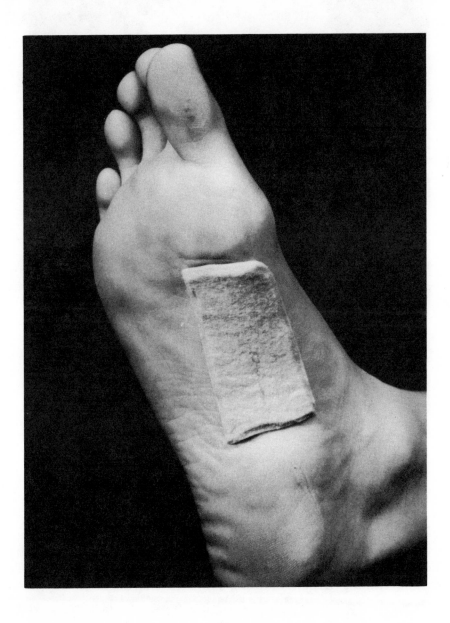

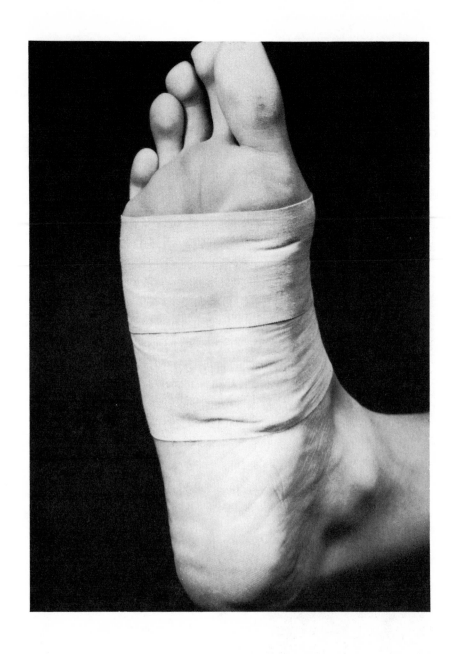

HALLUX LIMITUS AND HALLUX RIGIDUS
(Stiff Great Toe Joint)

Hallux limitus and hallux rigidus, stiffening of the great toe joint, are generally more common in male dancers than female because of the softer shoes they wear—the impact from jumps and leaps is greater. Among female dancers, however, the incidence of these painful conditions is greatest among teenagers. Again, as with so many dance injuries, hallux limitus and hallux rigidus are the result of repetitive shock and force to the great toe joint. The joint becomes inflamed and stiffens up, the result of which is "limited" motion (hallux limitus). Remember, as you rise on *demi-pointe*, if dorsiflexion (bending) of the great toe is restricted, your body weight shifts to the outside of the foot, which in turn will turn inward at the ankle joint. Then, not only do you have a painful great toe, but you are more prone to strains of the outer ankle, pain in the outer leg (peroneal tendinitis), and a general strain and weakening of the foot muscles. Finally, if the conditions that caused the limitus are allowed to continue then the joint may in fact become completely rigid (hallux rigidus), with the possibility of subsequent arthritic changes.

Diagnosis

The up and down motion of the great toe is limited and movement in general causes pain in the area of the first metatarsophalangeal joint. Getting from *demi-pointe* to *en pointe* is particularly painful and difficult to perform. The dancer will try to shift her

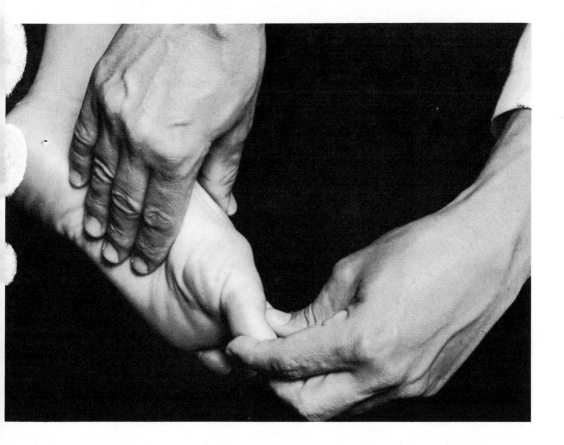

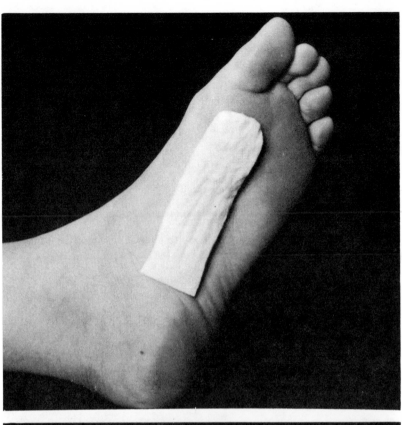

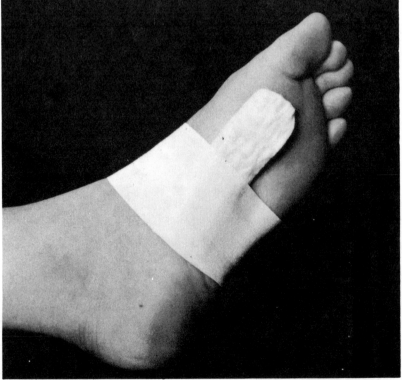

weight to the outer border of the foot in order to prevent any movement of the great toe. As a result fatigue is hastened. When you move the affected toe forcibly up and down, you notice a rough, irregular movement and sometimes a grating sensation. It is extremely important that treatment is begun early in the case of hallux limitus before the joint stiffens and professional care must be sought.

Treatment

Take three or four aspirin every four hours for three days, two every four hours thereafter, as needed, for the inflammation. Add a layer or two of sponge cushioning to your street shoes for extra protection, or wear wooden clogs to reduce joint movement. You may insert an adhesive-backed felt pad under and slightly behind the joint to reduce the impact against it. This is accomplished in the following manner:

1. Prepare the skin by painting with benzoin or spraying with pre-tape such as Tuf-Skin.

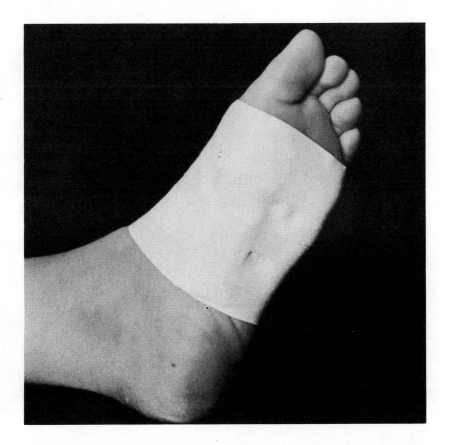

2. Cut out a pad one-eighth- or one-quarter-inch thick from adhesive-backed felt, approximately the length of the first metatarsal, and bevel on all sides, slightly more at the front.
3. Place this pad in position and strap with 1½-inch or 2-inch cloth tape.

In young dancers especially, if hallux limitus is allowed to go untreated, the condition may become so severe as to require surgery to restore joint movement. As results are often less than adequate, the dancer should begin treatment promptly and expediently. Several weeks rest, minimum, must also be included. Use crutches if you need them to keep pressure off the affected joint. Remember, you are the one most responsible for your well being: any form of reconstructive surgery is likely to leave the joint permanently weakened.

JAMMED OR SPRAINED GREAT TOE

A jammed or sprained great toe often results from constant pointe work or from direct injury with modern dancers who dance barefoot. The ligaments of the great toe joint may be sprained, the cartilage bruised, or the joint capsule stretched or torn. In general,

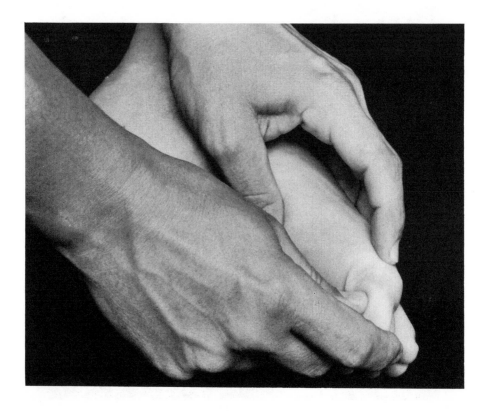

jammed toes are more common among ballerinas and sprained toes among modern dancers. Movement becomes limited and painful, especially at the interphalangeal joint.

Treatment

Take three or four aspirin every four hours for three days, two every four hours thereafter as needed. The application of a cold compress or ice massage three times daily for fifteen to twenty minutes affords additional relief. Wear wooden-soled clogs to minimize the movement of the great toe and, if needed, strap it in the following manner.

1. Paint the great toe with benzoin or spray with pretape such as Tuf-Skin.
2. Begin your strapping with two strips of one-inch *elastic* tape that are wrapped around the toe and cover the first metatarsophalangeal joint. These strips should overlap by approximately one-half.

STRAPPING FOR PAINFUL BIG TOE

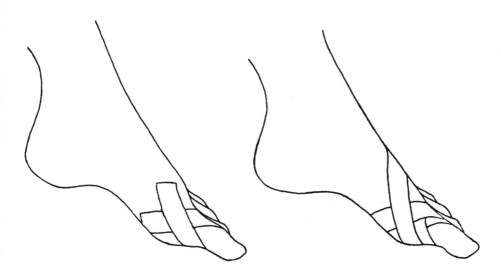

1. First strip of 1-inch elastic tape.

2. Second strip of elastic tape over laps the first by one-half.

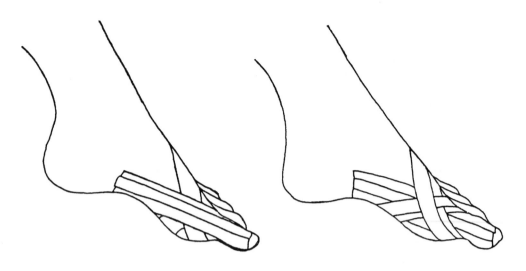

3. Three overlapping strips of cloth tape.   4. Second set of elastic strips in place.

3. Beginning at the tip of the great toe, apply three overlapping strips of *cloth* tape that extend back over the joint to a point roughly mid-way to the heel.
4. Complete your strapping with two more strips of one-inch elastic tape in the same manner as the first two, which come around the toe and cover the first metatarsophalangeal joint.
5. The entire strapping can now be anchored, if you wish, with two or three 1- or 1½-inch strips of cloth tape that are wrapped around the front of the foot, bottom to top, where the ends cross.

"FALLING OVER" THE GREAT TOE

A sudden and violent "falling over" the great toe, particularly during a series of quick steps, can result in a tear at the top of the joint capsule of the first metatarsophalangeal joint, where the great toe joins the foot. This type of forcible flexion injury is especially common in male dancers and those who are engaged in modern dance. Intense pain occurs at the time of injury, and you find it impossible to move the great toe up or down. The joint becomes inflamed and swollen.

Treatment

Ice will afford a degree of relief, ten to fifteen minutes three times daily. Aspirin assists in controlling the inflammation, three or four every four hours for three days, two every four hours thereafter as needed. Wear wooden-soled clogs to limit motion at the joint. After a week to ten days, depending upon the stability and condition of the joint, you should begin a series of passive, non-weight-bearing exercises. Do not expect full range of motion in the joint for six to eight weeks, however. Keep it as stable as possible during this time, strapping as necessary (see "Jammed or Sprained Great Toe" section for illustrations of this technique).

1. Paint the great toe with benzoin or spray with pretape such as Tuf-Skin.
2. Begin your strapping by placing two strips of one-inch *elastic* tape around the great toe and covering the first metatarsophalangeal joint. These strips should overlap by approximately one-half.
3. Beginning at the tip of the great toe, apply three overlapping strips of *cloth* tape that extend over the joint to a point approximately mid-way to the heel.
4. Complete your strapping with two more strips of one-inch elastic tape in the same manner as the first two, which come around the toe and cover the first metatarsophalangeal joint.
5. The entire strapping can now be anchored, if you choose, with two or three 1- or 1½-inch strips of cloth tape that are wrapped around the front of the foot, bottom to top, where the ends cross.

NEUROMA
(Benign Nerve Tumor)

A benign nerve tumor known as a neuroma may result from wearing pointe shoes that are too tight and forcibly squeeze the heads of the metatarsals together, damaging the nerves that pass between them. These benign nerve tumors occur most commonly between the third and fourth metatarsals, sometimes between the fourth and fifth, but only rarely between the second and third. As these neuromas may be confused with less serious conditions, metatarsalgia and metatarsal bursitis, for instance, read the following material very carefully, and consult the other pertinent sections.

Diagnosis

Initially you feel a burning sensation between your toes at the level of the metatarsal heads or just behind them. This burning sensation often radiates back toward the heel. Pain is usually noticed

71

only during activity or on weight bearing but eventually appears during periods of non-weight-bearing as well, with a shooting electric-like tingling sensation between the toes and into the foot. By this time you may also notice a numbness between the insides of the opposing toes or cramping in the foot when you wake up in the morning. *Demi-pointe* becomes especially painful, and you notice that the most immediate and effective relief from the discomfort simply comes from sitting down and removing your pointe shoes.

Perform this simple test. Squeeze the metatarsal heads together with one hand while pressing the suspected interspace (where you have felt the pain) with the other hand. A sharp, shooting, or electric sensation that runs from the immediate area of discomfort through the foot and into the leg is virtual proof positive that you have a neuroma.

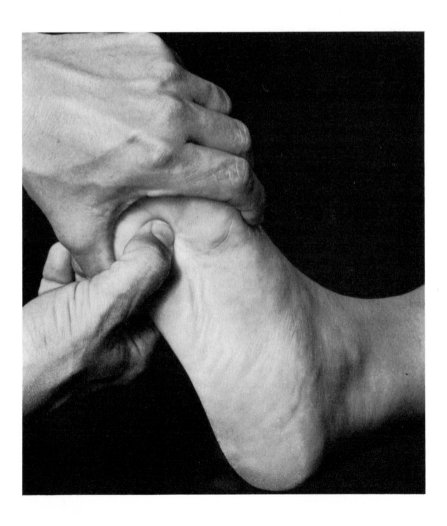

Immediate relief can be obtained from icing the area for twenty minutes three times daily. Three or four aspirin every four hours also may bring about a degree of symptomatic relief. Be certain to ice the area for at least ten minutes after class or performance. Finally, padding the area to remove the pressure of the two opposing metatarsals will prove beneficial in relieving the painful symptoms. If you are fortunate, the combination of aspirin, icing, and padding may bring about complete relief in two to three weeks. However, you must wear pointe shoes with a wider box, padding them and your street shoes as well if necessary. (For illustrations of this technique, see section on "Stress Fractures of the Metatarsals.")

1. Prepare the skin by painting with benzoin or spraying with pre-tape such as Tuf-Skin.
2. Cut two elongated rectangular strips from one-eighth- to three-eighths-inch adhesive backed felt that approximate the length and width of the two opposing metatarsals. For example, if the neuroma is located between the third and fourth metatarsals, then these shafts are padded. Round the corners of the pads and bevel on all four sides.
3. Attach below the shafts of the opposing metatarsals and strap into place with 1½-inch cloth adhesive tape.

Note: Some dancers have found that a simple plantar metatarsal pad which is placed beneath the shafts of the second, third, and fourth metatarsals works just as well. This pad is cut roughly in a heart shape and attached just beneath the heads of these metatarsals. Strap into place as described above. (See section on "Metatarsalgia and Anterior Metatarsal Bursitis.")

While surgical removal is the only "cure" for a neuroma, many dancers have discovered that the long-term use of padding (as needed) works quite nicely indeed. It is a good idea, however, if the condition persists but you do not elect to have surgery, to place three-eighths-inch felt metatarsal pads in all your shoes or have a good shoe repairman attach metatarsal bars to them. The felt pads must be replaced periodically, every three or four weeks usually, as they wear down.

The simplest way to make this felt insert is to attach the pad to a Spenco, Dr. Scholl, or Plastizote inlay that has been cut to the shape of your foot. (The insert with the metatarsal pad can be changed

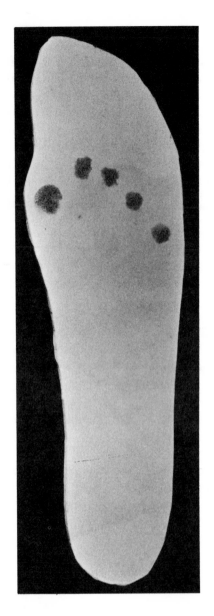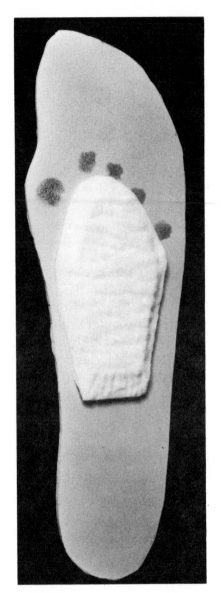

from shoe to shoe.) To determine the exact positioning of the pad requires a good impression of the metatarsal heads. This may be accomplished by inking the metatarsal heads with a felt-tipped pen or lipstick and standing immediately on the cut out insert, bearing down hard to transfer the impression. Another method of obtaining an accurate impression is to wear the insert for a week or so until the heads have been marked by pressure or their location is marked by

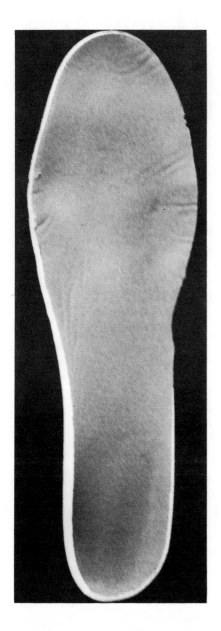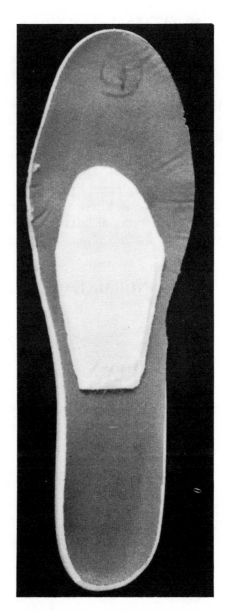

simple soiling. Attach a heart-shaped metatarsal pad of one-quarter-
or three-eighths-inch felt, beveled on all sides, just behind the im-
pressions of the metatarsal heads.

If all of these methods fail to bring about effective symptomatic
relief, then you should consult an orthopedist. The surgical removal
of a neuroma is a fairly minor procedure which should in no way
effect your ability to dance (no bones or joints are involved).

METATARSALGIA AND ANTERIOR METATARSAL BURSITIS
(Pain in the Ball of the Foot)

Repeated jumps and leaps on uneven or hard surfaces, even poorly constructed rehearsal room floors or stages, can lead to severe pain across the ball of the foot. These predisposing factors are complicated by pointe shoes that are too tight. The heads of the metatarsal bones or the bursae that cover them are bruised and may become inflamed. Dancers with particularly bony feet as well as those who try to avoid rolling by turning the foot in such a way that the great toe is lifted are more apt to develop metatarsalgia and anterior metatarsal bursitis. Jumps and leaps produce pain, as do *pliés*.

NORMAL METATARSAL ALIGNMENT

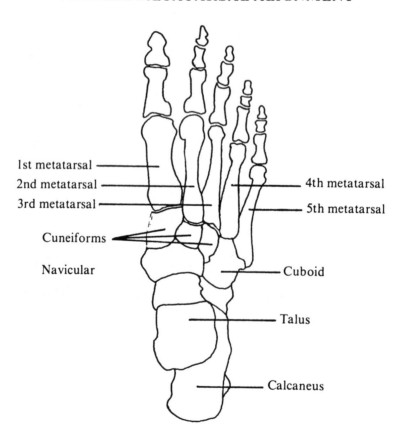

1st metatarsal

2nd metatarsal

3rd metatarsal

4th metatarsal

5th metatarsal

Cuneiforms

Navicular

Cuboid

Talus

Calcaneus

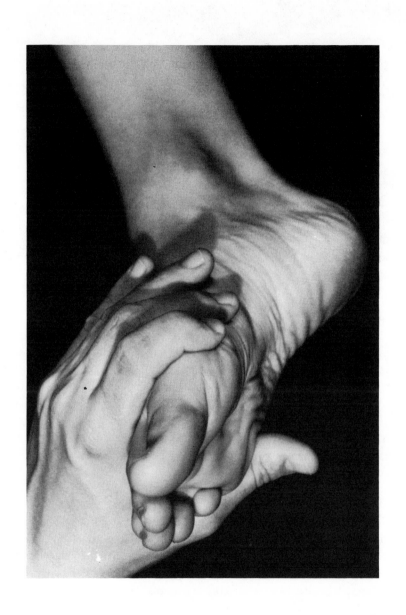

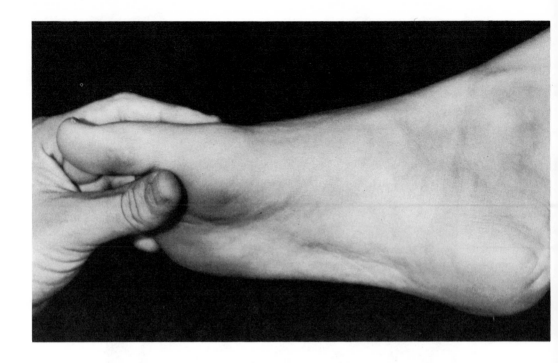

Diagnosis

Pain is elicited when the metatarsal heads are squeezed together or when individual metatarsal heads are pressed from the underside. If squeezing individual metatarsal heads together between the thumb and forefinger produces more pain than direct pressure from the ball of the thumb the chances are that you have anterior metatarsal bursitis. Otherwise you might expect metatarsalgia. The treatment for each is essentially the same.

Treatment

Deal with the inflammation by taking three or four aspirin every four hours for three days, two every four hours thereafter as needed. You may ice the area for ten to fifteen minutes two or three times a day for three days but change over to moist heat, (warm water soaks, whirlpool if available, or parafin baths) after three. If the condition is relatively mild and not so debilitating, you may find that the application of a plantar metatarsal pad will allow you to continue class or performance as the condition slowly improves. Remember, however, that this pad is no substitute for complete rest and a period of non-weight bearing.

1. Prepare the skin by painting with benzoin or spraying with pre-tape such as Tuf-Skin.
2. Cut and bevel a pad from quarter- or half-inch adhesive-backed felt that extends from the mid-foot region to a point just behind the inner three metatarsal heads and slightly winging the first metatarsal head. *Note:* This pad may slightly overlap the metatarsal heads but should not cover them.
3. Secure the pad with strips of 1- or 1½-inch tape, beginning at the

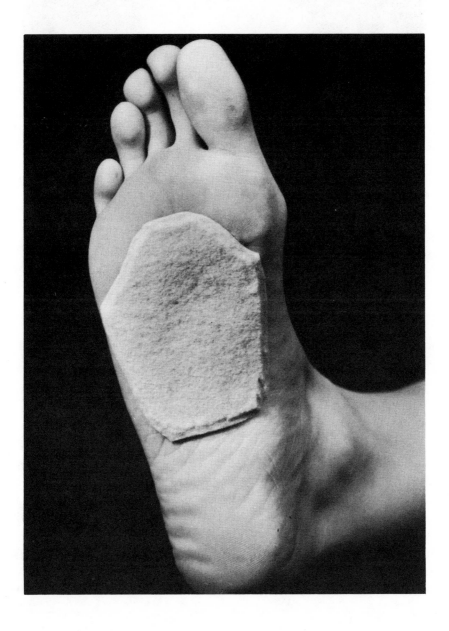

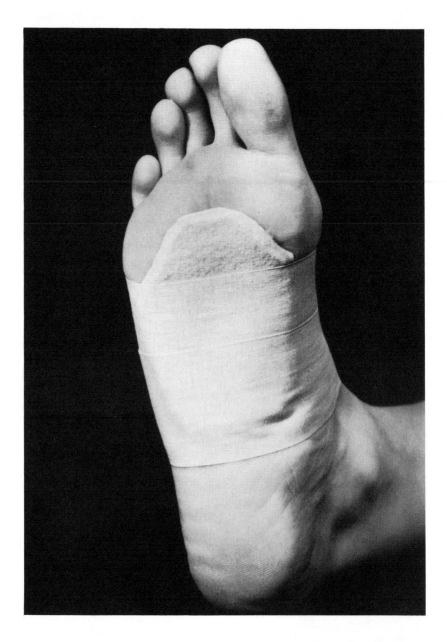

mid-foot and proceeding forward to the ball of the foot. Each succeeding piece of tape should overlap the former by one-half.

During the recovery period you will find that Dr. Scholl's exercise sandals or wooden clogs, if more practical, will provide a degree of relief. Do not wear high-heeled shoes until all symptoms have disap-

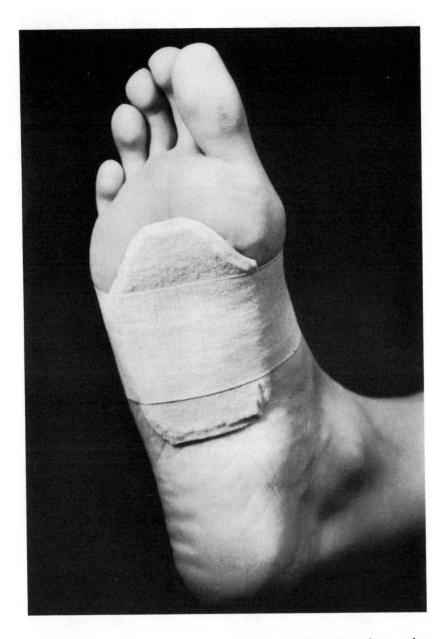

peared. Do not wear shoes with extremely flexible soles such as tennis or deck shoes, but add a layer or two of sponge padding to your street shoes. If you are dealing with a chronic case of metatarsalgia you may expect a recovery time of four to twelve weeks, depending upon the care you take. Do not rush the process by returning to class too soon. *Note:* If the pain you are experiencing is more

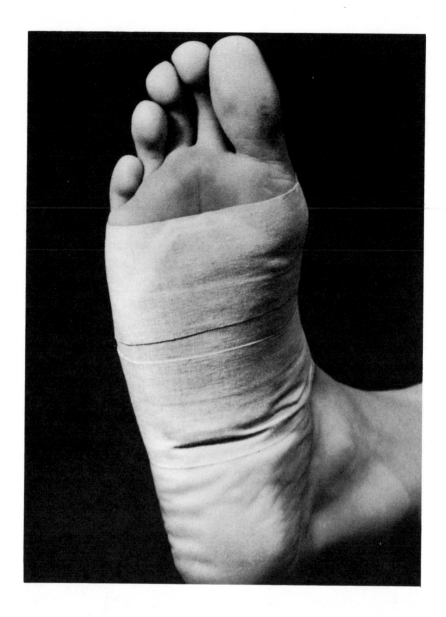

isolated than diffuse you may be dealing with a stress fracture of a metatarsal or a benign nerve tumor known as a neuroma, so check these sections in this book as well.

STRESS FRACTURES OF THE METATARSALS

Stress fractures of the metatarsal bones of the foot, most commonly involving the second metatarsal, are the result of the additive impact and shock of repeated jumps and leaps, as well as from the bending forces acting on the metatarsal shafts. The absence of adequate shock absorbing materials in pointe and ballet shoes or hard, unresilient dance surfaces predispose the dancer to this painful condition. Dancers who try to avoid rolling by turning their feet in such a way that the big toes are lifted are more prone to stress fractures of the metatarsals than are those who use correct technique.

Diagnosis

It is important to remember that stress fractures are not related to a specific traumatic event such as a twist or fall but develop over a period of time. In the early stages the pain experienced from a stress fracture may be vague, even dull. You find that you are able to "dance through" the discomfort without much difficulty. After a time, however, the pain becomes more intense, and jumps especially are aggravating and produce a sharp burning sensation at the level of the fracture. Pressing the area of the head of the metatarsal (in the ball of the foot) or along its shaft produces an excruciatingly painful response. Once the fracture has occurred, weight bearing of any kind becomes quite difficult.

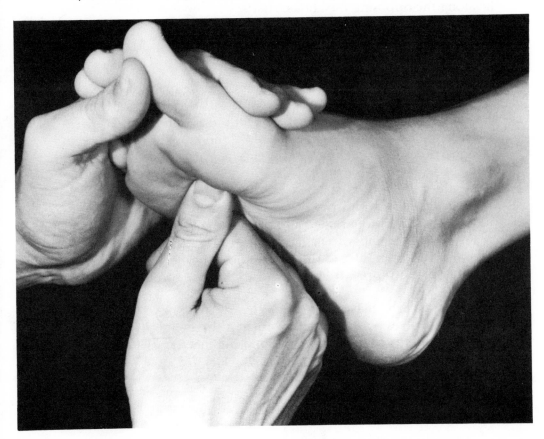

The pain produced by a simple hairline stress fracture will subside significantly with rest but will recur if you start back too soon. Take three or four aspirin every four hours for the first three days and two aspirin every four hours thereafter as needed. Icing the area for approximately ten to fifteen minutes at a time three times a day will greatly assist in reducing any swelling that might have occurred. If you must move about, wear wooden clogs to limit the motion in the metatarsal region. For more serious fractures you must restrict weight bearing altogether, using crutches for four to seven days. Once the stress fracture has healed, you should begin a regimen of exercise that strengthens the intrinsic muscles of the foot, including extra *battlements tendus* in class. You will want to add as much padding to your shoes as you can—Sorbothane, Spenco, or Dr. Scholl's cushion inlays are all fine. A thin layer in your pointe shoes is also recommended. If the fracture does not require casting, you will find that a degree of relief can be achieved by padding the foot with adhesive felt. Either one of two methods may be used.

Let us assume that it's the second metatarsal that is involved. The first method employs a U-shaped pad; the second, parallel pads that lie along the opposing metatarsal shafts.

METHOD 1

1. Prepare the skin by painting with benzoin or spraying with pre-tape such as Tuf-Skin.
2. Cut out and bevel from quarter- or three-eighths-inch adhesive-backed felt a pad in the shape of a "U," the wings of which extend up to a point just behind, or barely covering, the first and third metatarsal heads. You may have to experiment a bit with the depth of the hollow part between the wings.
3. Secure the pad with strips of 1½-inch or 2-inch cloth tape, beginning at the mid-foot region and proceeding forward to the ball of the foot. Remember to bring the ends of the tape from the bottom around the sides of the foot to the top, where they cross. Do not apply with pressure; simply wrap the tape around the foot.

The other method may prove equally as effective for you as the first. This one involves placing a quarter-inch or three-eighths-inch adhesive-backed felt pad along the two opposing metatarsal shafts.

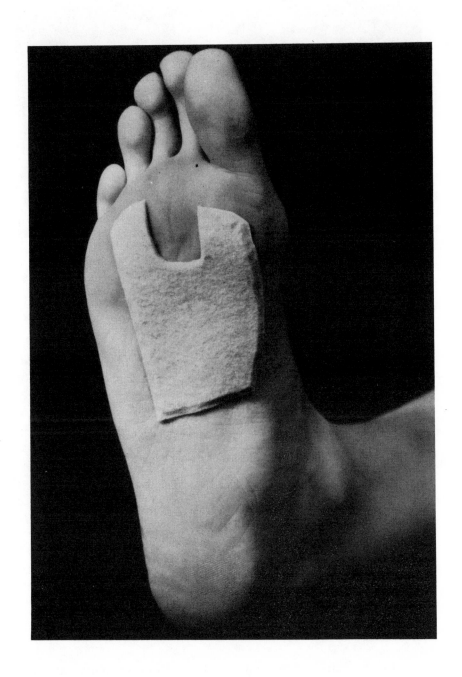

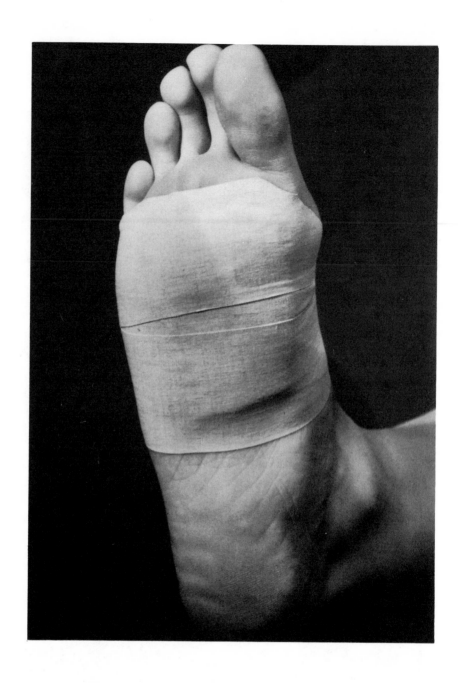

METHOD 2

1. Prepare the skin by painting with benzoin or spraying with pre-tape such as Tuf-Skin.
2. Cut and bevel two felt pads, approximately three-eighths- or one-

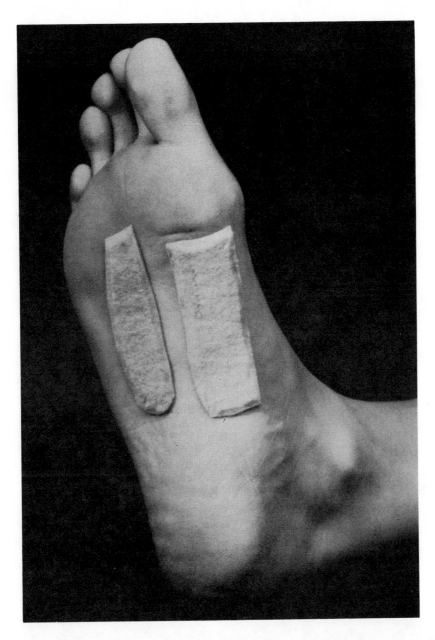

half-inch in width, the length of the first and third metatarsal shafts, from their respective bases in the mid-foot region to a point just behind or slightly covering their heads (in the ball of the foot). Remember, the first metatarsal shaft is shorter than the third, so the two pads will differ somewhat in length.

3. Strap these pads in place with 1½-inch strips of cloth adhesive tape.

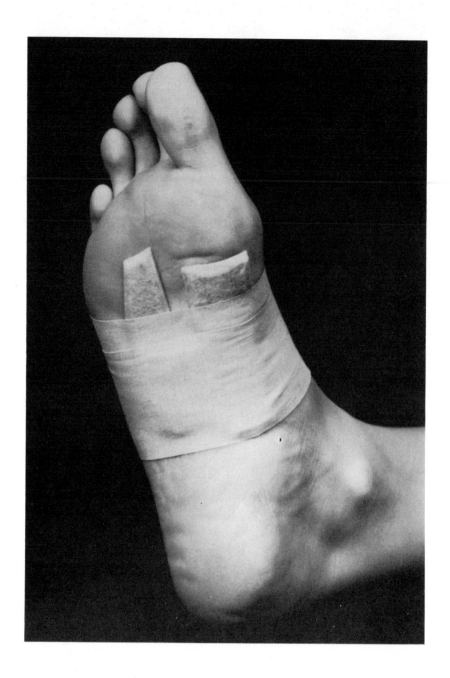

Remember, stress fractures are slow to heal and easily reinjured. Do not rush the healing process. Your patience will be rewarded by a greatly decreased healing time.

Arch pain not specifically related to plantar fasciitis or a strain of the flexors of the great toe (see below and following) may be due to a series of predisposing factors that have compounded to produce the discomfort. There is a general break down, as it were, of the supporting mechanisms of the long arch of the foot. Usually this break down is aggravated, even brought on, by hard, unresilient dance surfaces or a series of classes or rehearsals that include an unusually large number of jumps and leaps. You notice that once the pain has started you are probably carrying a disproportionate amount of your weight on the inner side of your foot, whether dancing, standing, running, or walking. The foot tends to pronate or turn in and downward. The arch is depressed. The muscles that support it have become weak, and the extra load is passed on to the ligaments binding the bony components of the arch. This causes the joints involved to separate very slightly, giving the effect and sensation of having "fallen." At some point during this course of events the muscles of your foot, and those that originate in the leg and control some of the movements of the foot and ankle, try to assist the strained ligaments. A spasm then often results because the muscles become too weak to do the job. *Note:* Dancers who try to turn out from the ankles by allowing the feet to roll in predispose themselves to this mechanism.

Remember, as dancers your calf muscles and posterior tibials are unusually tight and contracted owing principally to the very nature of classical ballet itself. Often you find that it is difficult to get your heels down in *petite allegro,* and *pliés* become difficult. When these muscles are allowed to become excessively tight, you notice that your legs cannot move freely over the feet and, biomechanically speaking,

MEDIAL(INNER)VIEW OF THE RIGHT FOOT

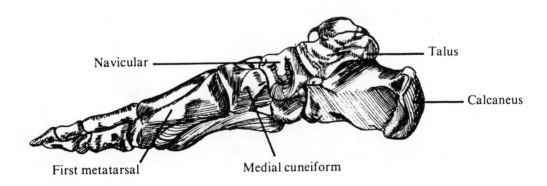

Navicular

Talus

Calcaneus

First metatarsal

Medial cuneiform

89

for normal balance you are not able to achieve the minimum of ten degrees of movement over the foot. When this movement is inhibited, an excessive strain is placed on the foot so that the intrinsic muscles are strained. An overuse syndrome of the leg may also result.

Diagnosis

Your feet become swollen (or at least they *feel* like they are swollen), ache, and fatigue easily. You begin to notice that the muscles in your legs also ache during activity and even during periods of rest. Usually there is a sharp pain elicited when you press the ball of your thumb into the high point of the arch; indeed, the entire length of the arch may be sensitive to pressure. Frequently there is accompanying pain across the ball of the foot as well.

Treatment

Many dancers have found that placing their feet in ice water after class or performance assists in reducing the swelling that may be present. Aspirin will do much to relieve any inflammatory process that has developed—two or three every four hours as needed. Further relief may be obtained by padding the foot with adhesive-backed felt, changing daily for a week or more. This padding, if properly applied, will not only relieve the strain on the arch but will also encourage normal muscle balance and equal weight distribution. You may also find that wearing commercial arch supports in

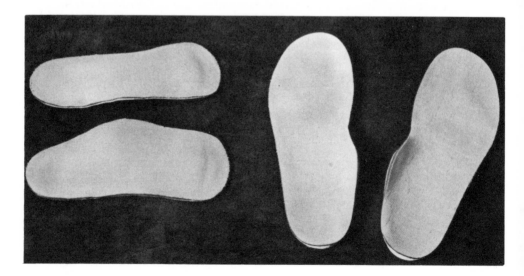

your street shoes, Dr. Scholl's 610's or Lynco Biomechanical Supports, for instance, will prove extremely beneficial.

1. Prepare the skin by painting with benzoin or spraying with pre-tape such as Tuf-Skin.
2. Cut out and bevel on all sides a quarter- or three-eighths-inch thick adhesive-backed felt pad that is shaped approximately half-moon-shaped. It should extend in length from a point just be-

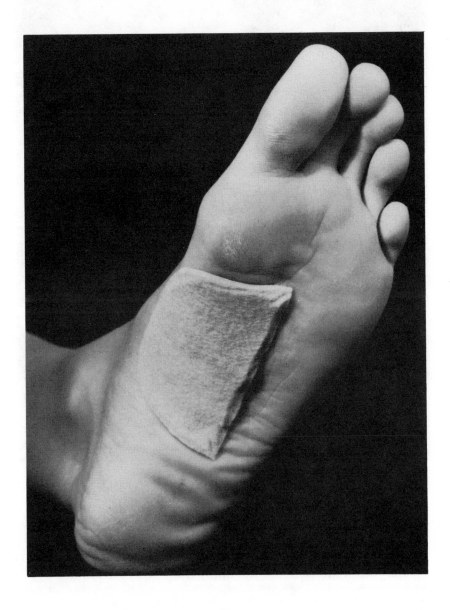

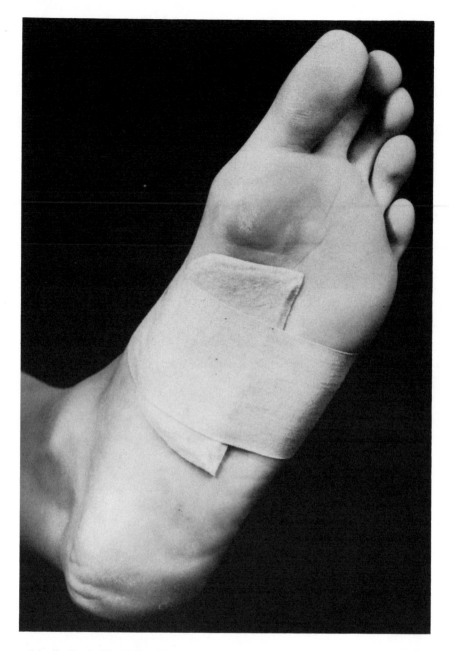

hind the ball of the big toe to a point just beyond the high point
of the arch of the foot.

3. Attach this pad to the foot and strap it in place with strips of 1½-
   inch cloth tape, beginning at the back (heel end) of the pad,
   proceeding forward. Each strip overlaps the former by approximately one-half. *Note:* Do not apply these straps with pressure but

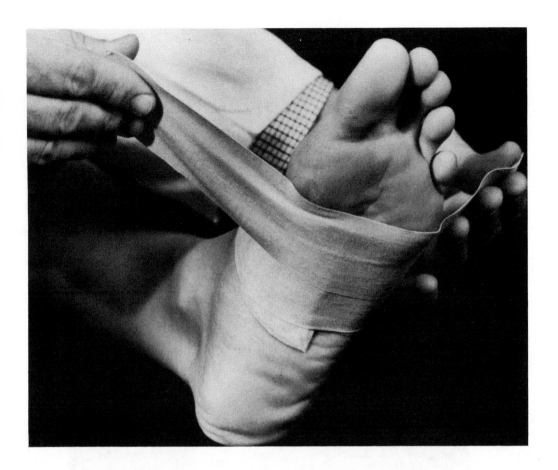

simply wrap them around the sides of the foot from bottom to top. Cloth tape will give somewhat, but if the strapping is too tight, you should peel back the strips and lay them over again with less pressure than previously.

You may find that it is necessary to continue the use of this padding for a period of two to four weeks before the pain has subsided completely. The dark, moist environment created by the strapping may lead to skin irritation. Therefore keep the skin as dry as possible while the pad is in place and go without it over weekends, if possible. Once you are back in class, you can begin to strengthen the arch by doing extra *battements tendus,* but be especially careful to keep the arch supported during *barre* or center practice. Do not allow it to relax at the end of any movement of *plié* or *fondu.* Ask your teacher or trainer to give you a series of exercises that will strengthen the muscles of the foot and always take extra care to maintain proper technique.

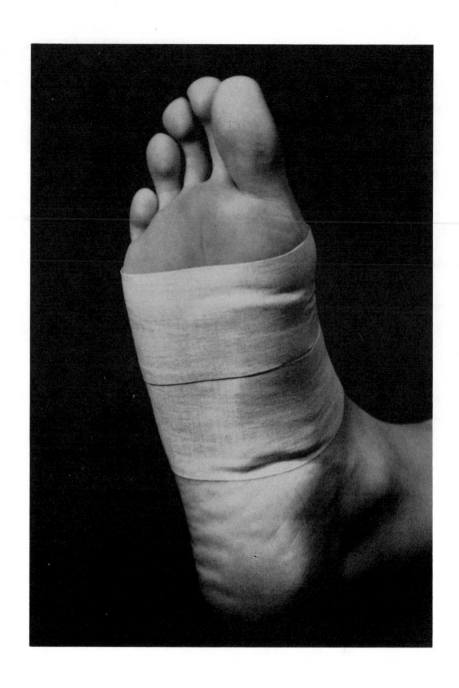

DORSAL EXOSTOSIS
(Bump on the Top of the Foot)

A bony enlargement on the top of the foot, which may be either
congenital or acquired as the result of a chronically jammed first

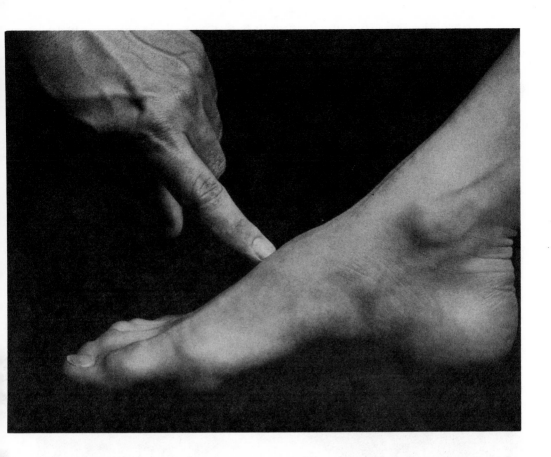

metatarsocuboidal joint, can be rather a painful problem for a dancer. Friction and rubbing from footwear, everyday or dance, will irritate the bump which then becomes red and swollen. A bursa which forms over it to protect the enlargement also becomes irritated and thereby compounds the problem. The pain that results may be quite exquisite indeed. If you have flat or pronated feet, you are more apt to have these dorsal exostoses.

Treatment

Icing the bony enlargement several times each day for up to twenty minutes at a time affords a degree of relief. Take three or four aspirin every four hours for up to three days, and two every four hours thereafter as needed. If common sense has not already dictated it, wear shoes that do not rub or irritate the bump. You may also want to pad the area in this fashion.

1. Bevel the sides of a precut bunion pad or cut and bevel your own pad from eighth-inch adhesive-backed felt. The aperture in either should be just larger than the bump you are protecting.
2. Place the pad in position over and around the bump and strap into place with several strips of one-inch cloth adhesive tape. Replace as needed.

Once the inflammation has been checked, you may find that protecting the area on a regular basis with moleskin or molefoam will keep it from becoming irritated. *Surgery is contraindicated because the scar it leaves could prove a problem in and of itself.*

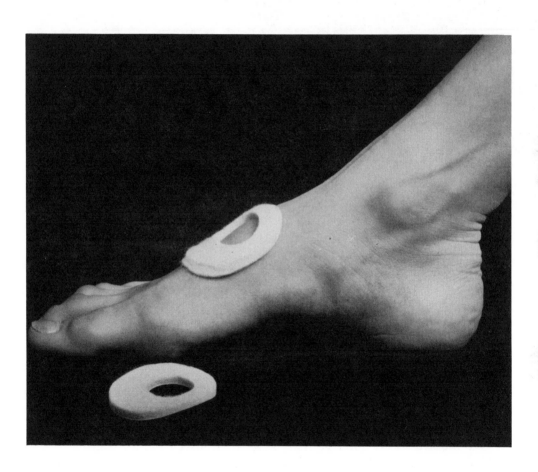

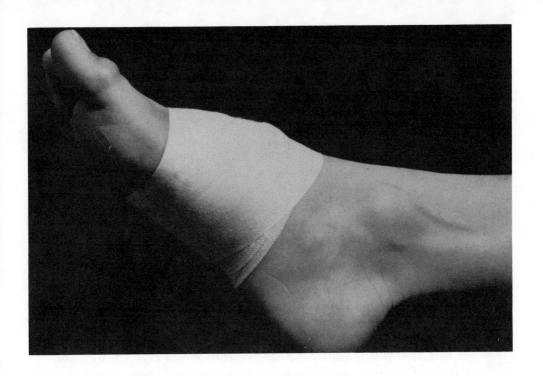

JONES FRACTURE
(Avulsion of the Base of the Fifth Metatarsal)

Dancers are especially vulnerable to fractures, sprains, and strains when there has been a change to a more rigorous routine, or when they are over-fatigued or "out of balance." Jones fracture, or the cracking or breaking away of the base of the fifth metatarsal bone, is a common injury of this sort. A violent or uncoordinated movement

JONES FRACTURE

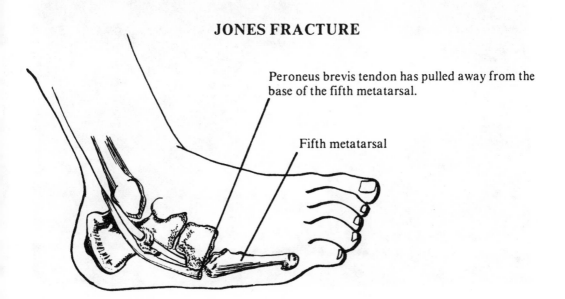

Peroneus brevis tendon has pulled away from the base of the fifth metatarsal.

Fifth metatarsal

of the peroneus brevis muscle, which inserts into this bone and assists in raising the outer border of the foot, is usually the cause.

Diagnosis

More times than not you actually hear a snap or pop when the base of the fifth metatarsal has been damaged. There is intense pain and swelling at the site of injury. Turning the arch of the foot upward, actively or passively, produces intense pain.

Treatment

If the base of the fifth metatarsal is not completely broken through, you may be able to keep the foot securely strapped and relatively pain free for three to four weeks while the area heals. You may even be able to continue class on a very limited basis after two weeks. If there is a true avulsion, however, your orthopedist may want to put you in a walking cast. Typically it will take up to three months before the area is strong and symptom free, but there should be no permanent damage that will continue to bother you.

In the event of a simple crack or hairline fracture, or for supportive taping after the cast has been removed, this technique should prove helpful:

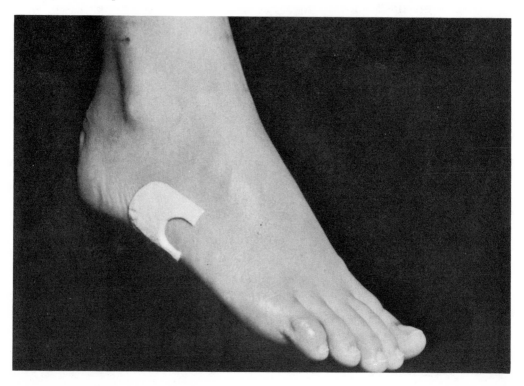

1. Prepare the skin by painting with benzoin or spraying with pre-tape such as Tuf-Skin.
2. Cut off the front rounded aspect of a commercial felt bunion pad and bevel on all sides. (You may also cut your own U-shaped pad from eighth-inch adhesive-backed felt.)
3. Place this pad in position directly *behind* the base of the fifth metatarsal, where the bone juts out a bit, with the prominence within the wings of the "U" of the pad. *Note:* You should actually *push* the pad in place, in the direction of the little toe.
4. Take strips of half or one-inch cloth tape and form a basket-weave design on the outside of the foot. The first strip begins on the outside of the foot just in front of the heel and is applied with a bit of forward pull—the heel end of the tape is held in place with the thumb of the other hand.
5. Take a shorter strip of tape which is anchored to the sole of the foot and brought around to the top-center of the foot.

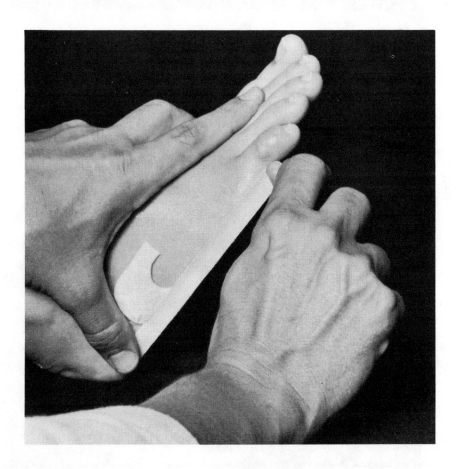

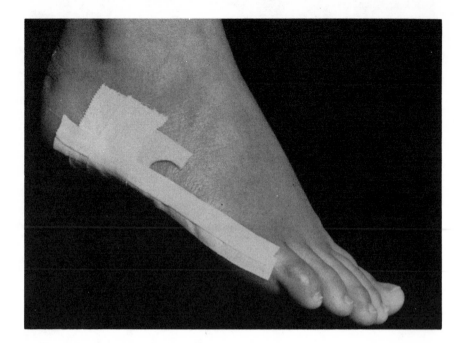

6. Now apply another long strip overlapping the first by approximately two-thirds, and a second short strip overlapping the former by one-half.
7. Continue with this strapping until you have reached a point approximately 1½ inches beyond the base of the fifth metatarsal. Several anchor strips wrapped around the foot, bottom to top, will further secure your basket-weave strapping.

Because the area is still vulnerable to reinjury, even after the discomfort has totally subsided, you should take special care *not to perform moves that roll the foot under.*

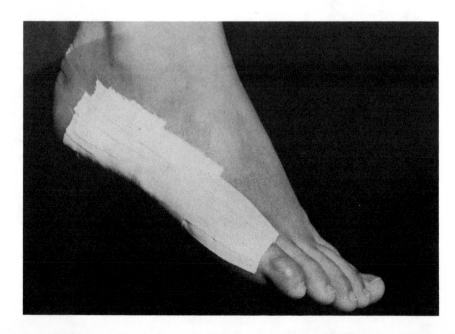

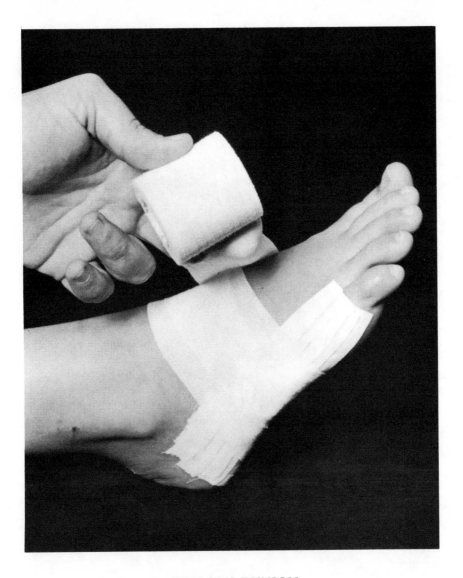

TAILOR'S BUNION

A tailor's bunion, or bunionette, is a congenital enlargement of the head of the fifth metatarsal often made more prominent by a metatarsal shaft that bows outward. Because the tailor's bunion protrudes from the outer aspect of the foot, it is subjected to abnormal pressure. A bursa may form over the joint to protect it, but finally it swells with fluid and becomes inflamed. The area surrounding the head of the fifth metatarsal becomes hot, red, and swollen and extremely painful to the touch. Tight pointe shoes can make the condition almost unbearable.

TAILOR'S BUNION WITH ENLARGED FIFTH METARSAL HEAD AND BOWED SHAFT

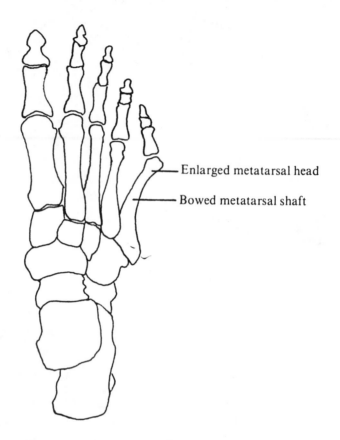

— Enlarged metatarsal head

— Bowed metatarsal shaft

(compare with diagram of "Normal Metatarsal Alignment")

Treatment

To deal with the immediate discomfort of an inflamed tailor's bunion begin a regimen of ice and aspirin. Ice the area two or three times daily for fifteen to twenty minutes. Take three or four aspirin every four hours for three days, two every four hours thereafter as needed. Finally, protect the bony enlargement from excessive abnormal pressure by padding with felt.

1. Prepare the skin by painting with benzoin or spraying with pre-tape such as Tuf-Skin.

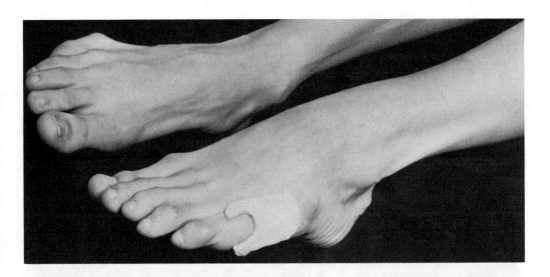

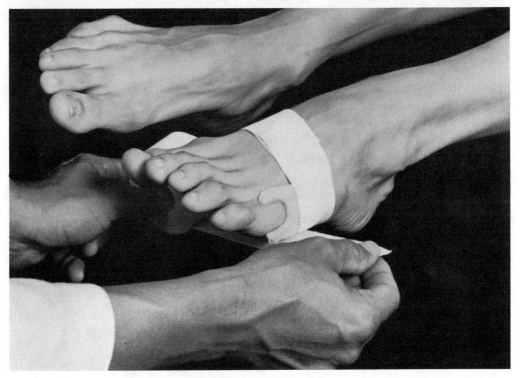

2. Cut away the front of a commercial felt bunion pad and bevel on all sides. The "U" created should cradle the bony knob. Some dancers prefer to leave the front of the pad intact, but they must bevel it more on the front than the sides or back.

3. *Or:* Cut your own pad from quarter-inch adhesive-backed felt.

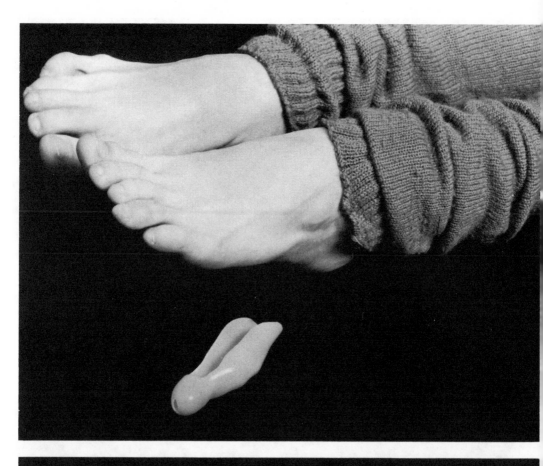

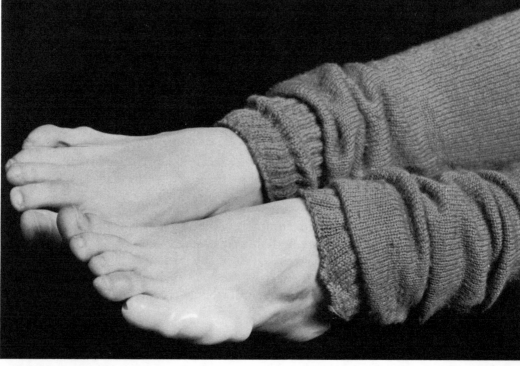

Start by cutting an egg-shaped piece of felt, which you bevel on all sides. Cut a pocket in the pad almost through but not quite. You can enlarge the pocket with your thumb or forefinger for a better fit.

4. Place the pad of choice in position and secure with 1- or 1½-inch cloth adhesive tape.

In the future, to prevent a badly inflamed bursa, you may want to pad the area routinely or simply cover the bony eminence with moleskin. A latex bunion shield may suffice.

SUBLUXED CUBOID

A severe pain along the outer border of the foot or on the upper outside surface at the level of the fourth and fifth metatarsals, often sudden in onset, may indicate a partial subluxation (dislocation) of the cuboid bone. You notice that if you press along the peroneus brevis tendon that a painful response is elicited, one that may even extend up to the level of the ankle or above it. Pressing the cuboid from beneath almost always produces a sharp, electric-like pain. More times than not the condition is brought on after long workouts on hard, unresilient surfaces in which jumps and leaps are involved. *Ronde de jambes* become especially painful.

Treatment

If not too severely dislocated the cuboid can often be coaxed back into its proper alignment with the application of a cuboid pad and strapping. A certain amount of relief can be achieved if nothing else.

LATERAL (OUTER) VIEW OF RIGHT FOOT

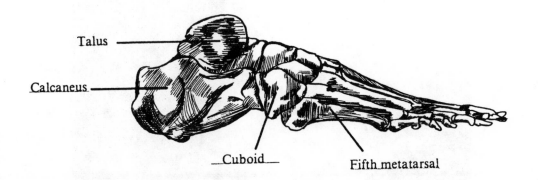

Talus

Calcaneus

Cuboid

Fifth metatarsal

If after a week or ten days the discomfort has not significantly improved, then you may have to seek professional assistance in having the cuboid manipulated. First, however, try this pad and strapping combination.

1. Prepare the skin by painting with benzoin or spraying with pre-tape such as Tuf-Skin.
2. Cut out and bevel on all sides an oval pad from eighth- or quar-

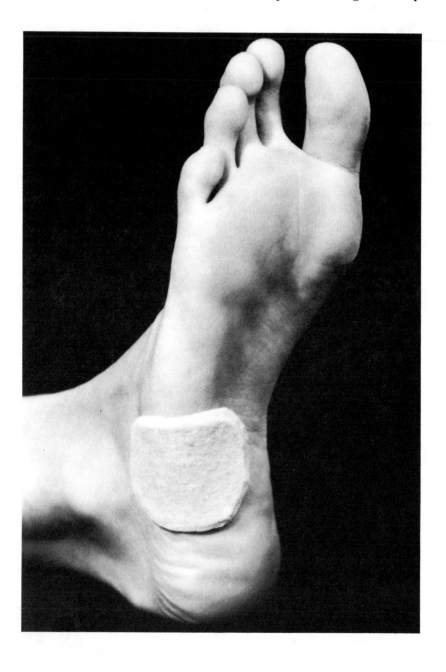

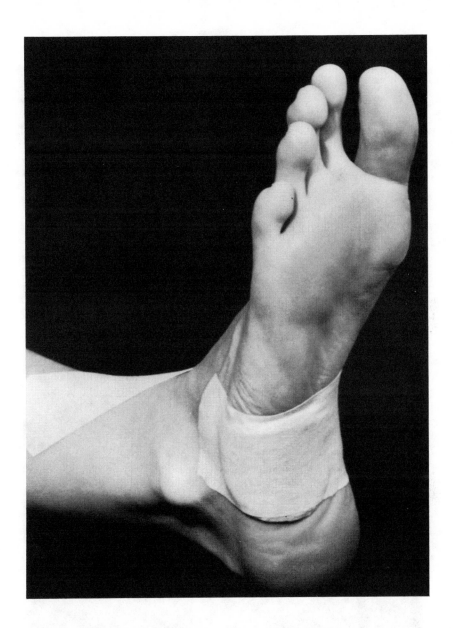

ter-inch adhesive-backed felt that extends from the center of the sole of the foot under and around the side of the cuboid. *Note: The outer aspect of this pad that wraps around the foot should be beveled thinner than the inner side.*

3. Secure the pad with a piece of two-inch cloth adhesive tape beginning on top of the foot and pulling it over the cuboid pad with a little pressure, around the inner side, over the top, to a point just over the shin, about four to five inches above the ankle.

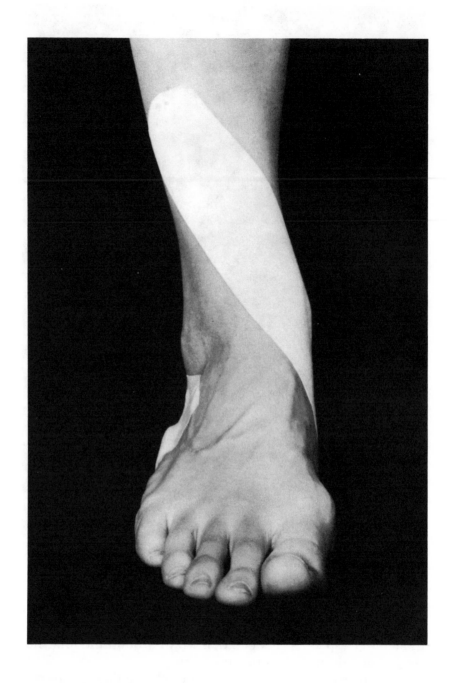

If the pad and strapping are properly applied, you should receive immediate symptomatic relief. Change the pad daily, if necessary, for a period of up to one week.

EXTENSOR TENDINITIS

Occasionally a ballerina will experience pain on top of her foot. There is no dorsal exostosis (bump) present, but inflammation and swelling are noted. The skin over the long tendons on top of the foot is puffy. Mild to moderate discomfort is experienced when the toes are lifted. The mechanism that is responsible for this condition is usually quite simple: your pointe shoes are too tight and cause an undue amount of pressure and friction on and against the extensor tendons, so they become inflamed.

EXTENSOR TENDONS ON THE DORSAL (TOP) ASPECT OF THE FOOT

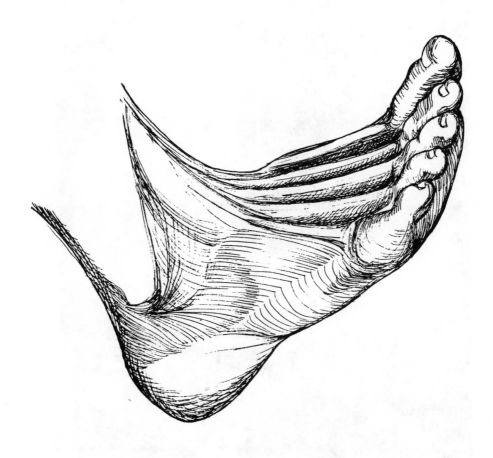

Ice the painful area for fifteen to twenty minutes after class. Take three or four aspirin every four hours for several days, or until the symptoms have diminished, two every four hours thereafter as needed. Reduce the friction against the extensor tendons by covering the top of your foot with a layer of moleskin and strapping it into place with 1½-inch cloth tape. You may also try to line the inside top of your pointe shoes with moleskin or molefoam. Hereafter you must take care to buy pointe shoes that afford more room over the top of the foot.

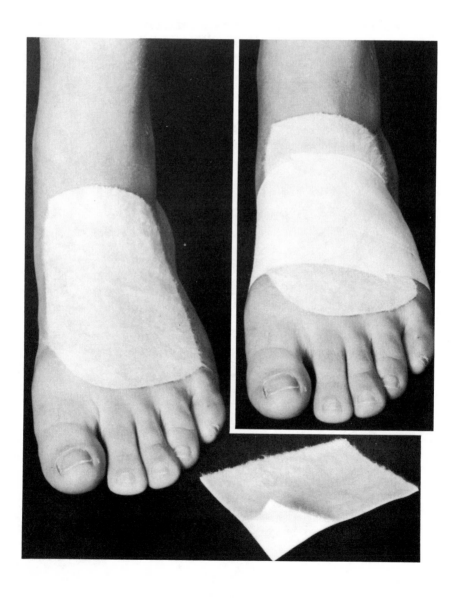

The plantar fascia is a tight band of dense connective tissue that lies deep in the foot and stretches from the front lower aspect of the heel bone to a point just behind the toes. It is the strongest ligament in the body and assists in maintaining the structure of the foot, particularly the long arch. It is also one of the most common sites of dance injury. Dancers whose feet are pronated, or roll in, are predisposed to strain of the plantar fascia, as are those who land from

DEEP ASPECT OF THE SOLE OF THE FOOT SHOWING THE PLANTAR FASCIA

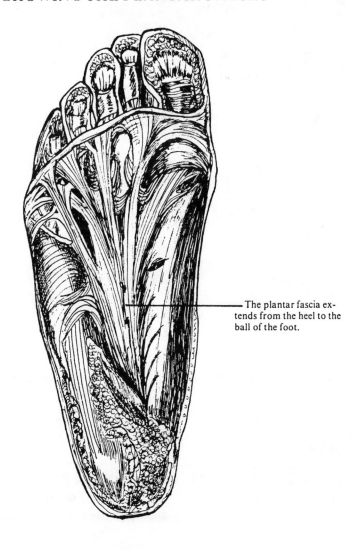

The plantar fascia extends from the heel to the ball of the foot.

jumps or leaps on the balls of their feet. Hard unresilient floors certainly increase the eventuality of this painful condition. Remember, landing from jumps, properly or improperly, triples, even quadruples, the forces that pass through the foot and ankle. This repetitive shock in and of itself can lead to plantar fascial strain. Once injured it is very slow to heal. *Note:* Plantar fasciitis and strain of the plantar fascia may occur coincidentally with heel spurs, so also consult that section as well. Treatment is essentially the same.

STRAIN OF THE PLANTAR FASCIA

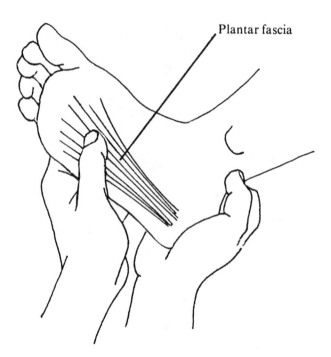

Plantar fascia

Plantar fascial strain is one cause of arch pain and "weak feet."

Diagnosis

The arch of the foot becomes extremely painful and may swell. There is a point on the heel where the plantar fascia attaches that is exquisitely painful to direct upward pressure, approximately one

112

STRAIN OF THE PLANTAR FASCIA AND HEEL SPUR SYNDROME

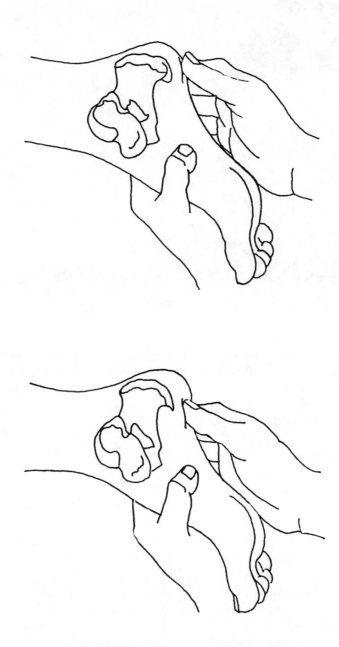

The pain caused by heel spur syndrome is elicited near the front of the heel.

Strain of the plantar fascia results pain approximately 1-inch from the back of the heel.

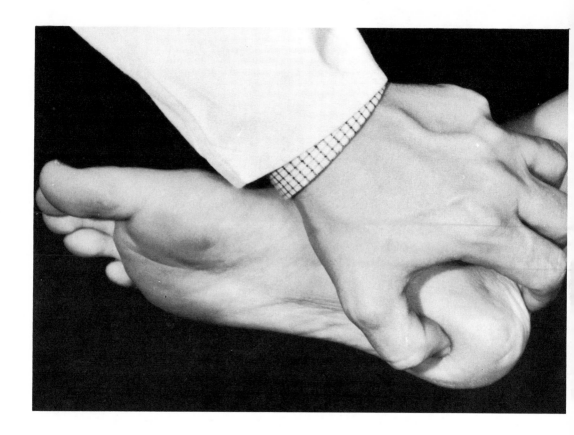

inch from the back edge of the heel. You usually experience a great deal of pain and tightness in the foot when you first get up in the morning, but soaking your foot in warm water for five to ten minutes will most likely relieve the discomfort. *Relevé* especially causes an increased degree of pain.

Treatment

Ice the heel and arch of the foot fifteen to twenty minutes three times a day as long as the pain persists. Take three or four aspirin every four hours for three days, two every four hours thereafter as needed. Some therapists recommend at this stage a gentle stretching of the plantar fascia, usually within two or three days after the symptoms appear. This is accomplished by forcibly moving back and forth beneath the arch a rolling pin or a hard ball, three to five minutes, three times daily. A commercial wooden foot exerciser works just as well if you have one.

Initially you should add extra padding to your street shoes—Spenco or Dr. Scholl's foam inserts, Sorbothane if you can obtain it.

114

Heel lifts are also recommended, three-eighths to half-inch. In the early stages, however, when the pain is most intense, the application of a Low Dye strap, with or without a felt support pad, affords a great deal of relief and speeds up the healing process. In fact, if you follow up with the ice-aspirin-strapping technique, assuming you have not allowed the condition to go too far, you may notice symptomatic improvement within forty-eight to seventy-two hours.

1. Prepare the skin by painting with benzoin or spraying with pretape such as Tuf-Skin.
   2. *Optional.* Cut out and bevel on all sides a quarter- or three-eighths-inch adhesive-backed felt pad which covers the foot from the front of the heel to a point just behind the inner three metatarsal heads, winging it just a bit under the first metatarsal head. Attach to the sole of the foot. (See section on "Metatarsalgia and Anterior Metatarsal Bursitis.")
3. Cover the back of the heel with a two by two-inch gauze or Telfa pad to prevent undue irritation at this point.
4. The foot should be dorsiflexed (bent) to a ninety degree angle and held thus while the straps are being applied. Take a strip of one-inch cloth adhesive tape and measure the distance from a point mid-way down the fifth metatarsal shaft on the outside of the foot to a point which approximates the middle of the shaft of the first metatarsal on the inner side of the foot. Cut in advance three strips this length.
5. With the foot dorsiflexed at a ninety degree angle, the first strip is applied. With *firm* pressure, begin on the outside of the foot, pulling the tape tightly around the heel and, as you approach the mid, inner side of the foot, forcibly bend down the big toe as you secure the end (the subject should resist this movement by keeping the toe up).
6. Apply a second strip of one-inch tape in the same manner, this one overlapping the first by one-half. The second strip should just reach but not cover the insertion of the Achilles tendon.
7. The third strip comes over the first two, angling up toward the top of the foot.
8. Take strips of two-inch elastic or cloth tape and begin at the front end of the foot where your first strips are attached and apply them from side to side, attaching them to the cloth strips. These are also applied with pressure and cover the felt pad (if you have applied one) on the sole of the foot.
9. Take one more strip of one-inch cloth tape and bring it around

115

LOW DYE STRAP

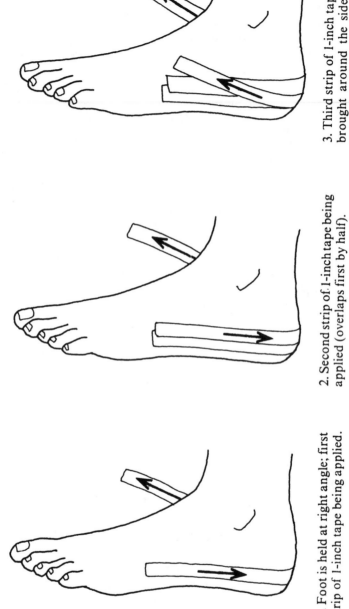

1. Foot is held at right angle; first strip of 1-inch tape being applied.

2. Second strip of 1-inch tape being applied (overlaps first by half).

3. Third strip of 1-inch tape is brought around the sides of the foot from the heel.

the sides of the foot to cover and secure the edges of the elastic tape.

10. Finally, secure the entire strapping with two or three strips of two-inch cloth tape that are wrapped around the foot, bottom to top. These should *not* be pulled on but simply laid around.

This pad-strapping combination may be worn effectively for two or three days but should be replaced regularly to allow the foot a chance to "breathe," daily if practical. Keep the foot dry while the pad and strapping are in place.

When you return to class, remember that extra *battements tendus* are good for developing strength in the arches and thereby decrease the likelihood of such painful conditions as plantar fasciitis or general arch strain.

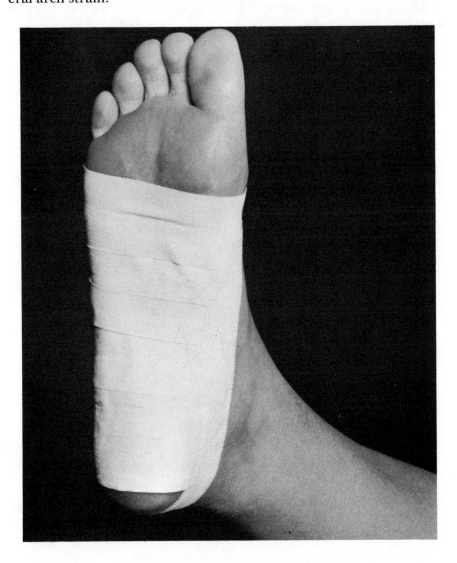

HEEL SPURS

Heel spurs are bony growths or calcium deposits on the lower front aspect of the heel bone at the point of insertion of the plantar fascia. They seem to occur more commonly among dancers with pronated or flat feet and often are noted coincidentally with a chronic case of plantar fasciitis. Most authorities now believe that the pain that results is actually the result of an inflammed bursa and no. from the spur itself.

Diagnosis

A very deep tenderness is detected by direct pressure to the front aspect of the heel bone. There are pain and stiffness when you first get up in the morning or during prolonged periods of weight-bearing, whether dancing or walking. Occasionally the pain may radiate from the heel into the sole of the foot. (See also sections on "Plantar Fasciitis" and "Dancer's Heel.")

HEEL SPUR SYNDROME

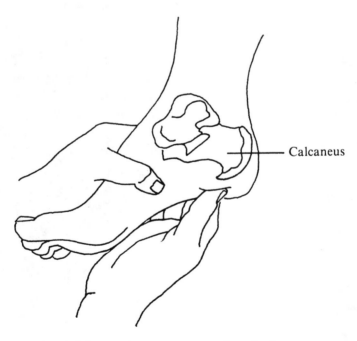

Calcaneus

A painful response to pressure against the front
aspect of the heel may indicate heel spur syndrome.

Treatment

To relieve the painful symptoms of heel spurs you should treat the condition like any form of bursitis. Take three or four aspirin every four hours for three days, two every four hours thereafter as

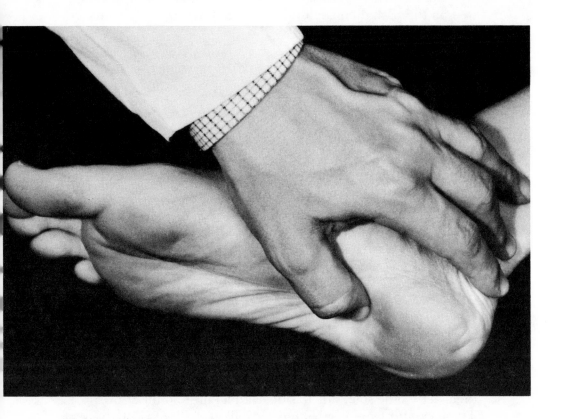

needed. You may find that applying an ice pack directly to the area for up to twenty minutes brings about symptomatic relief. Some sort of additional support in your street shoes may also prove beneficial, Dr. Scholl's inlays or Lynco Biomechanical supports, for instance. These inserts will relieve the strain on the plantar fascia. A double layer of sponge insert will also provide additional relief. Initially, however, you will want to pad and strap the foot in the following manner.

1. Prepare the skin by painting with benzoin or spraying with pre-tape such as Tuf-Skin.
2. Cut and bevel a pad from eighth- or quarter-inch felt that ex-

tends from the heel to a point that approximates the mid-foot area.

3. Place this pad on the foot and press against it until you locate the exact point of pain. Mark the area with a felt-tipped pen and cut a hole in the pad just larger than the painful area. Another way to accomplish this is to mark the spot on the heel with lipstick and step on the pad, then cut away the area that receives the impression.
4. Attach to the skin.

Next, apply a Low Dye strap (see above).

1. The foot should be dorsiflexed (bent) to a ninety degree angle. Take a strip of one-inch cloth tape and measure from the bony prominence on the mid-shaft area of the fifth metatarsal on the outside of the foot to a point that approximates the mid-shaft of the first metatarsal on the inner side of the foot. Cut three strips this length.
2. Beginning on the outside of the foot, pull on the first strap with a bit of pressure as you round the heel. Before you attach it to the inner side, forcibly bend the big toe against resistance.
3. Apply a second strip in the same manner, overlapping the first by one-half. This strip should be just below the attachment of the Achilles tendon but does not touch it.
4. The third strip is brought around both sides of the heel and attached to the top of the foot.
5. Finally, take strips of two-inch elastic or cloth tape and apply them across the sole, side to side, with a fair amount of pressure. These extend from just behind the ball of the foot to the back of the heel, covering the pad that you have already attached. Each one overlaps the former by one-half.
6. Anchor these strips of elastic tape with one final strip of one-inch cloth tape that comes around the foot, covering the top edges.
7. If you like, you may now strap two-inch cloth strips around the mid-foot region for extra support. These come from bottom to top and are applied with mild pressure.

You can leave this pad and strapping in place for two or three days, but keep the foot as dry as you can. If there is any sign of itching or irritation, remove the pad for twenty-four hours or more. You should achieve symptomatic relief within a week to ten days.

BRUISED HEEL
(Calcaneal Periostitis, Inferior Calcaneal Bursitis, or Compressed Fat Pad)

A heel bruise is the result of repetitive and severe compression of the heel pad that covers the heel bone on its under surface, or of the underlying bursa or membranous covering of the heel bone. The condition is more common among dancers with bony feet that have little protective padding and may be brought on suddenly—coming down extremely hard from a jump, for instance—or simply from overuse or repetitive shock.

Fat pad beneath the calcaneus

Diagnosis

You experience severe pain on the under, mid-back side of the heel on weight bearing of any kind. This pain increases with leaps and jumps. The area is sensitive to direct or lateral (squeezing) pressure.

Treatment

Take three or four aspirin every four hours for up to three days

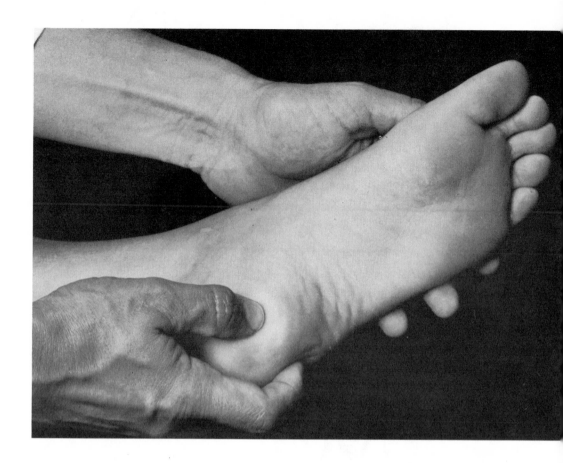

for the inflammation, two every four hours thereafter as needed. Ice the heel for fifteen to twenty minutes three times daily. Wear an extra layer of sponge padding in your street shoes until all symptoms disappear. Finally, if you are dealing with what appears to be mainly soft tissue and fat compression instead of inflammation of the bone lining or bursitis, this strapping will provide a degree of relief.

1. Prepare the skin by painting with benzoin or spraying with pre-tape such as Tuf-Skin.
2. Apply a strip of one-inch cloth tape under the heel from a point just in front of the heel on the outside of the foot (say one-half to three-quarters of an inch) to the corresponding point on the inside of the foot. Take care not to cover the attachment of the Achilles tendon with this strip or the next one.
3. Now apply the next strip of one-inch cloth tape from the inside to outside, around the heel.

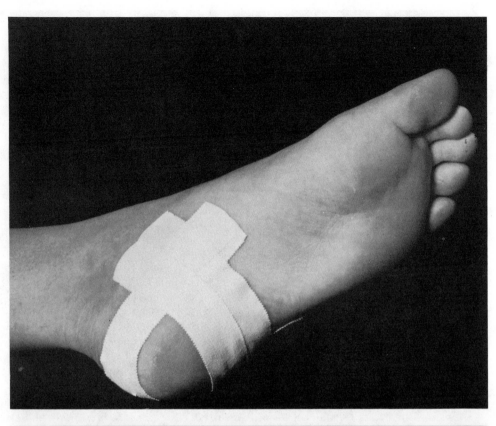

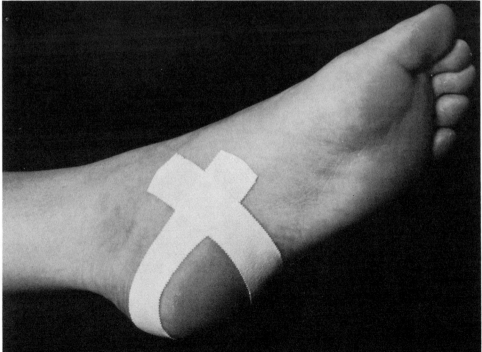

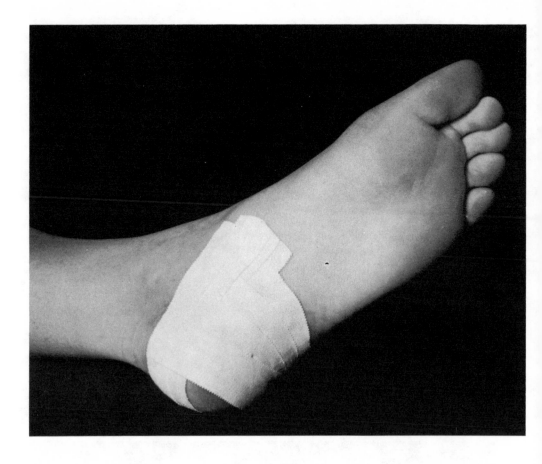

4. The third strip runs parallel to the first and overlaps it by one-half.

5. A final strip across the sole from outside-in completes the basket weave design.

This sort of heel strapping works quite well for a number of "mystery pains," including a bruised heel pad, so do not hesitate to try it. You may change the strapping daily and continue using for as long a period as is necessary. Ice and aspirin are used as needed.

DANCER'S HEEL

Dancer's heel is the painful result of excessive pointe work on hard, unresilient floors. Researchers believe that it is caused by an inflammatory response secondary to actual trauma to the calcaneotalar joint (where the ankle joins the foot). The simple act of

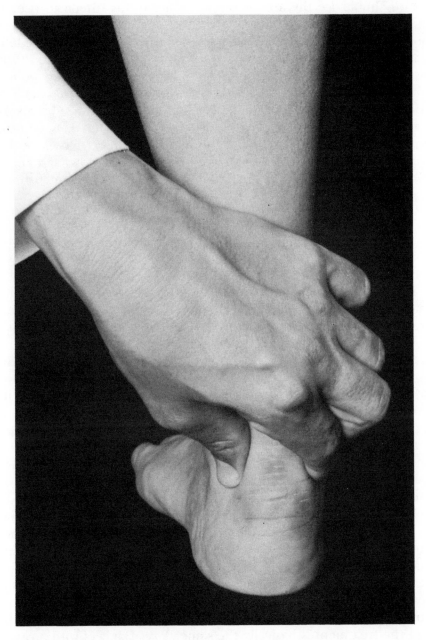

pointing the foot brings on severe pain in the area of the Achilles
tendon, but deep to it, at the level of its insertion in the calcaneus.
The inflammation causes a severe pain at the back of the ankle every
time the foot is pointed.

Treatment

You should ice the area three times a day for fifteen to twenty minutes for up to three days. Take three or four aspirin every four hours for three days, two every four hours thereafter as needed. You can try a Low Dye Strap (see section on "Plantar Fasciitis") for symptomatic relief and stability. *Note:* Dancer's heel makes pointe work very difficult to accomplish, so in order to maintain your balance you must flex (bend) the knee a little until the pain subsides. If symptomatic relief is not achieved within a week to ten days, consult an orthopedist. It is possible that you may have an extra bone at the back of your heel which you were born with, known as an *os trigonum.* It is a condition that cannot be relieved without professional intervention.

HAGLUND'S DEFORMITY AND POSTERIOR CALCANEAL BURSITIS

Haglund's deformity, or "pump bump," as it is more commonly known, is an abnormal ridge of bone at the back of the heel. You may have been born with it and had it all your life, or it may have developed in response to constant and unrelenting pressure against the back of your heel. If the condition is congenital you usually do not become aware of it until excessive friction and pressure have taken their toll. A bursa forms over the bump of bone to protect it. Pressure irritates this bursa as well, however, and it swells with fluid, making the "pump bump" seem even larger than it actually is. Eventually, if the source of friction is not removed, the walls of the bursa and the skin over it thicken and harden. The discomfort you feel is usually the result of the inflamed bursa and not always irritation of the bone itself.

If the discomfort is more at the *center* of your heel than to the side, at the point where the Achilles tendon inserts into the heel bone, then you probably have *posterior calcaneal bursitis.* This is an inflammation of the bursa that lies between the tendon and the skin. If the pain is just to the side of center, and the area is raised and hard, then you probably have a Haglund's deformity. However, either condition is brought on or aggravated by pointe shoes that are too tight and the treatment is basically the same. *Note:* Dancers with a cavus type foot (extremely high arch) which does not flatten enough when they walk or dance and those who have very low arches seem more predisposed to Haglund's deformity and posterior calcaneal bursitis than those with "normal" arches.

126

Diagnosis

You feel a burning or aching sensation at or around the "bump." The pain may be so exquisite that if the condition is left untreated you may find that the lightest touch of your finger or even the pressure of a bed sheet can be extremely painful. The only shoes that you are able to wear comfortably are open-heeled, such as wooden clogs.

Posterior calcaneal bursitis can be confused with Achilles tendinitis. Squeeze the tendon just above the point where it inserts into the calcaneus. If you have an inflamed posterior calcaneal bursa, there will be a more painful response at this point than with Achilles tendinitis, whereas any form of *movement* tends to aggravate an inflamed Achilles tendon more than an inflamed bursa.

Treatment

The object of treatment is to remove pressure from the irritated area. If you are successful at this, the inflammation can be controlled and the swelling will disappear, although it might still take two to three weeks or more. First, if common sense has not already dictated it, you should wear open-heeled shoes or clogs for everyday purposes. Do not wear any footwear that presses against the back of

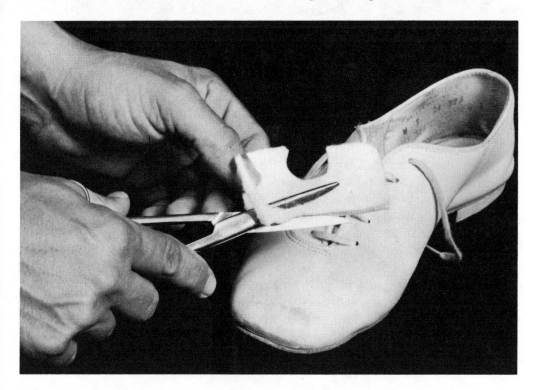

your heel until all symptoms have subsided. Icing for fifteen to twenty minutes several times a day will assist in reducing the localized swelling. You should take three or four aspirin every four hours for three days, and two every six hours thereafter as needed. A simple inflammatory condition should respond quite well to these measures alone. If there is still some discomfort and open-backed footwear is impractical, insert a three-eighths- or half-inch heel lift of felt or sponge rubber in your street shoes and cover the irritated area with a layer of moleskin. You may also want to line the backs of your shoes with several layers of moleskin or molefoam. Some dancers have found that splitting the backs of their pointe shoes and sewing in elastic will effectively reduce the pressure against the heel during class or performance.

For an extremely painful Haglund's deformity or posterior calcaneal bursitis you will need to protect the irritated area with an eighth- or half-inch adhesive-backed felt pad cut in an oval shape or with one or two beveled bunion pads.

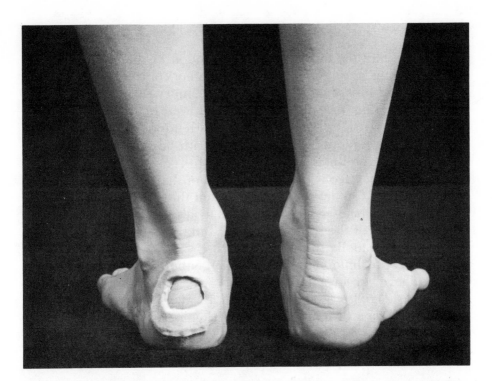

1. Prepare the skin by painting with benzoin or spraying with pre-tape such as Tuf-Skin.
2. Cut out an oval piece of felt and bevel on all sides.
3. Cut out a hole or a pocket in the center of this pad, whichever is more comfortable for you, and place it over the swollen, irritated area. This pad should completely surround without touching the sensitive portion of the heel; you may have to experiment a bit with placing the pad. (Some dancers have found that filling the aperture with wisps of cotton or lamb's wool further protects the heel.)
4. Strap into place with cloth adhesive tape.

If you do not have any adhesive-backed felt, you may use a precut felt bunion pad or two that have been stuck together. Either one is perfectly adequate for the job.

Surgery

Most orthopedists generally agree that heel surgery for dancers is not a good idea and try to avoid it. Be wary of any doctor who recommends a surgical procedure, especially on your first visit, and always seek a second opinion.

ACHILLES TENDINITIS

The Achilles tendon is the largest tendon in the body and, like other tendons, is quite inelastic and does not contract. The onset of Achilles tendinitis, a very common dance injury, may be sudden and without warning, or it may develop over a period of time. Dancers with extremely tight or narrow Achilles tendons are more predisposed to this condition than are those with flexible, thick tendons. (The Achilles tendon is usually three-eighths to one-half inch wide.) Repetitive shock from jumps and leaps on hard floors, sickling or rolling out, or forcing turnout, all hasten the onset of Achilles tendinitis. Ball-to-heel "stage running" may also lead to an inflammatory condition of the Achilles tendon, and the pain that results may cause you to walk flatfooted.

Improper technique that has resulted either in a weakened quadriceps above, or in a weak foot below, certainly predisposes the dancer to Achilles tendinitis. In the former instance you should begin a regimen of quadriceps strengthening exercises, and in the latter, extra *tendus* in class are especially beneficial (you should spend ample time to carry the stretch to the tips of the toes).

Diagnosis

You usually notice soreness along the entire length of the Achilles tendon, localized swelling, and severe pain in *relevé* especially. You

ACHILLES TENDINITIS

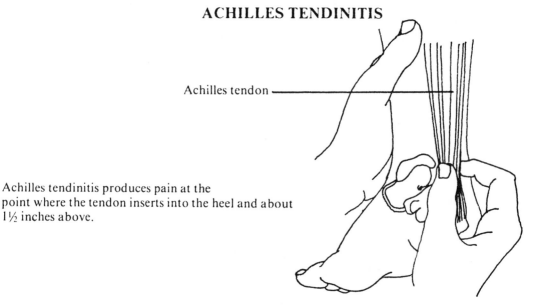

Achilles tendon

Achilles tendinitis produces pain at the
point where the tendon inserts into the heel and about
1½ inches above.

130

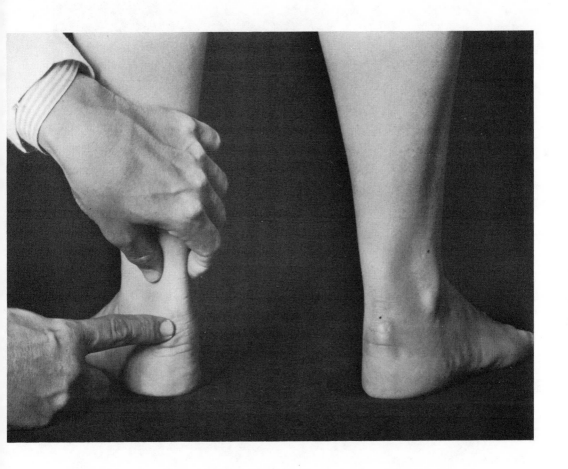

probably also notice that the pain is most intense when you first get up in the morning but improves as the day goes on. You get a false sense of confidence because in the early stages you are able to "dance through" the pain; however, six or eight hours later the discomfort can become quite intense indeed.

The most acute area of pain is usually about 1 ½ to 2 inches above the point where the tendon inserts into the heel. But if you start squeezing the tendon just above where it attaches to the heel, proceeding upward to the calf muscle, you will probably find another area of pain just where the tendon joins the muscle. You may have already noticed a "cracking" sound in the back of the heel when you move your ankles. *Note:* Unlike other tendons the Achilles tendon is not enclosed in a synovial sheath; rather, it is surrounded by connective tissue known as paratenon. Thus the term tenosynovitis does not apply to the Achilles tendon.

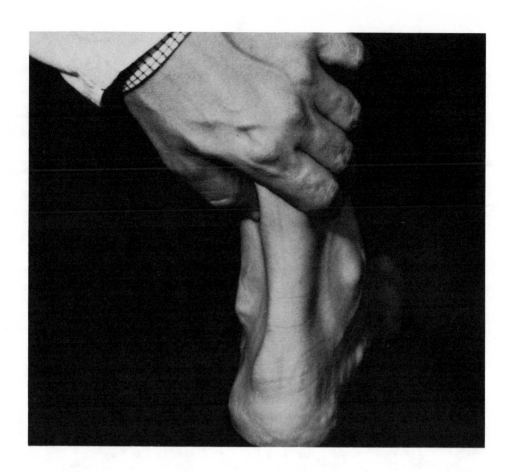

Treatment

Even with complete rest—no classes, no performances—it may take up to three weeks for the pain to subside. Icing the Achilles tendon at least three times a day for fifteen to twenty minutes will help reduce any swelling and inflammation that are present. Take three or four aspirin every four hours for three days, and two every four hours thereafter until the symptoms subside. Keep the leg elevated when you are at rest. Insert half-inch heel lifts in all your shoes, pointe shoes included (although you may only be able to dance comfortably with quarter-inch). As soon as you are ready to return to class on a limited basis you must stretch the Achilles tendon for at least ten minutes before each class. It is also a good idea to stretch it for ten minutes before you go to bed at night.

Stretching the Achilles Tendon: An excellent method for stretching the Achilles tendon is accomplished by standing three or four

feet from a wall with your hands flat against it. Lean forward, keeping your heels flat on the floor. Hold the length of your body straight for ten seconds. Push yourself back to an erect position, then lean forward again for a total of ten, ten second repetitions. You can increase the stretching effect by moving back from the wall at six-inch intervals.

Here is another method. Sit on the floor with your legs straight in front of you, knees locked. Bend the toes back as far as you can and hold for ten seconds. Ten repetitions are necessary. Then, using a towel, pull the foot forcibly toward your head, as far as possible. Hold for ten seconds and repeat ten times.

In addition to specific stretching exercises such as those recommended above, be certain that all forms of *demi-plié*, especially in first position, are a part of your daily routine. When your knees are bent, the heels *must* be on the ground. *Battements fondus* are also excellent for promoting elevation.

Initially, however, if the pain from your Achilles tendinitis is quite intense, you may need to strap the tendon in one of the following ways.

METHOD 1

1. Prepare the skin by painting with benzoin or spraying with pre-tape such as Tuf-Skin.
2. Sit on the edge of a table with your feet dangling loosely as the tape is applied. Stay relaxed.
3. Place two 1½-inch anchor straps of cloth adhesive tape just behind the ball of the foot, taking care not to pull them on too

133

ACHILLES TENDON STRAPPING

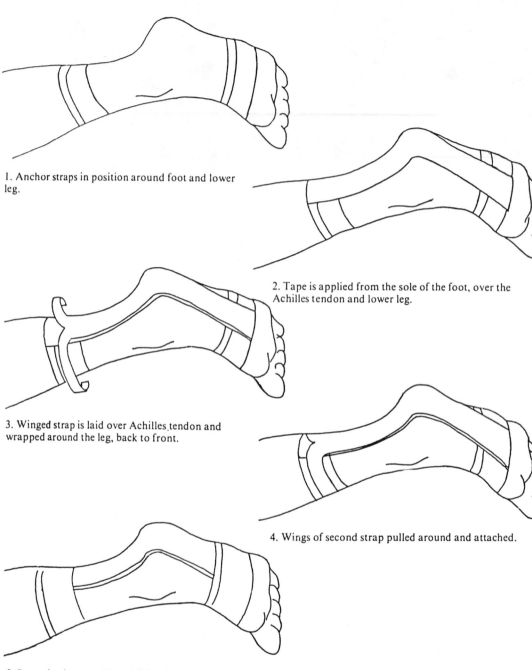

1. Anchor straps in position around foot and lower leg.

2. Tape is applied from the sole of the foot, over the Achilles tendon and lower leg.

3. Winged strap is laid over Achilles tendon and wrapped around the leg, back to front.

4. Wings of second strap pulled around and attached.

5. Strapping is secured by additional anchors around foot and lower leg.

tightly; simply wrap them around, the second strap overlapping the first by one-half.

3. Next, apply two or three 1½-inch straps about four to six inches above the ankle bones; these should also overlap by one-half.

4. Take a two-inch strip of cloth adhesive tape and attach it to the anchor straps on the foot, *lay* it along the sole, over the heel, and up the back of the calf to the anchor straps there. *Note:* Allow for just a slight amount of "play" in this strap, up to but no more than half an inch. Remember that the foot should be completely relaxed when you apply it.

5. Now take a second strip of two-inch tape, this one six to eight inches longer than the first, and split the upper end down the middle for about five inches. Apply this strip in the same manner as the first except that you bring the winged pieces around the sides of the leg and secure.

6. Finally, anchor the strapping top and bottom with three or four strips of 1- or 1½-inch tape, again *wrapping* (not pulling) them around.

To prevent the strapping from irritating the skin over the Achilles tendon, attach a layer of Telfa pads or gauze to the sticky side of the tape to reduce the "pulling" sensation. This strapping may be worn comfortably and effectively for several days and replaced as needed. Take care that the underlying skin does not become irritated. It is best, however, to replace the strapping daily.

Another method of strapping that is a bit more complicated, but more supportive for a severe inflammatory condition, is applied in this manner.

METHOD 2

1. Prepare the skin by painting with benzoin or spraying with pre-tape such as Tuf-Skin.

2. Lie flat on a table or on the floor, face down, while the strapping is applied. At the top of the calf attach three anchor straps of 1½-inch cloth tape, starting *below* and working up toward the knee, each overlapping the former by one-half.

3. Next, place anchor straps around the foot, starting at the ball of the foot and working back; three 1½-inch straps should be sufficient.

4. Bend the knee slightly by placing a book between the front of the ankle and the table; the foot should be pointed *slightly*.

135

ACHILLES TENDON STRAPPING: ALTERNATE METHOD

1. Anchor straps in position around leg and foot.

2. First strip of tape, applied from the sole of the foot over the Achilles tendon and leg

3. Second strip of tape applied from foot to leg, fanning outward.

4. Third strip of tape closes the gap between the first two strips.

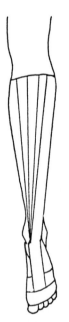

5. Fifth strip of tape in position.

6. Crimping tape over Achilles tendon.

7. Appearance of Achilles tendon strapping before securing.

8. The strapping completed.

5. A two-inch cloth tape support strap is now applied, beginning at the anchor on the foot and continuing up the back center of the calf. *Note:* This strap is attached to the anchors only, not to the skin itself.
6. Apply individual strips of 1½- or 2-inch cloth tape in a fan-like fashion, each one overlapping the former by one-half, again attaching them only to the anchors.
7. When the back of the calf has been completely laid-over with strips of tape, pull them together by crimping at the level of the Achilles tendon. In effect what you have done is to create a second, supporting tendon.
8. Finally, you must anchor this support, beginning at the metatarsal heads (or ball of the foot). Apply strips of 1½-inch cloth tape, each overlapping by one-half, over the ankle and up the leg. *Note:* If you have developed some expertise with taping, you may do this directly from the roll, crossing the ankle in a figure-eight pattern. It is safest and most effective for the novice, however, to proceed with individual strips.

With either technique of Achilles tendon strapping you have effectively limited the ankle to approximately ninety degrees motion by supporting and restricting it. *A final warning:* if you feel any tingling or numbing in your foot or calf, you have most likely applied your straps too tightly and the entire support must be removed *immediately,* then reapplied.

ANKLE SPRAINS

The ankle joint is made up of three bones: the *tibia* (inner leg bone) and *fibula* (outer leg bone), which together to form a mortice (groove or slot) into which the *talus* (ankle bone) snugly fits. Movement at this joint is in two directions only, up and down. The surfaces of the bones that form the ankle joint are covered with articular cartilage that allows for smooth movement in either direction. Holding the joint together are two principle sets of ligaments. On the inner aspect of the ankle is the three-part deltoid ligament, the stronger and more stable. It is infrequently injured. The bones of the outer aspect of the ankle joint are attached by three individual ligaments which are quite prone to injury. These ligaments, in order of the frequency in which they are stretched or torn, are: the *anterior talofibular ligament,* which attaches the lateral malleolus (outer ankle knob) to the front of the talus; the *calcaneofibular ligament,* which

LATERAL (OUTER) ANKLE LIGAMENTS

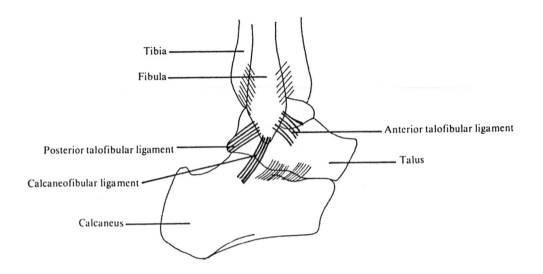

Tibia

Fibula

Posterior talofibular ligament

Calcaneofibular ligament

Calcaneus

Anterior talofibular ligament

Talus

DELTOID (INNER) ANKLE LIGAMENT

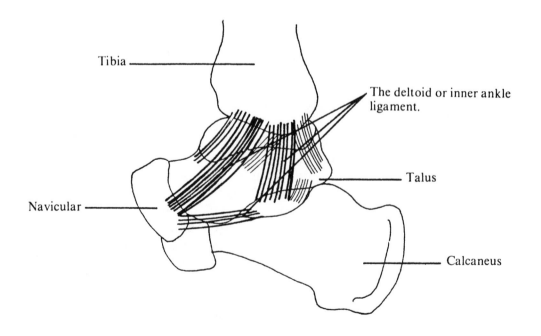

Tibia

The deltoid or inner ankle ligament.

Talus

Navicular

Calcaneus

attaches the talus to the calcaneus (heel bone); and the *posterior talofibular ligament,* which attaches the lateral malleolus to the back of the talus.

You should be aware that sickling weakens the outer ankle ligaments because of the unusual strain placed on them (the result of poor technique or inadequate training). In sickling, the inner arch of the foot is improperly held inward, with the pointe down and in, and the heel bone turned outward. Properly, when the foot is *en pointe,* your ankle joint is bent (plantarflexed), with the inner arch of the foot and heel forced in a forward direction. Such movements as *emboité,* when you sickle, greatly conduce to outer ankle weakness and muscle strain. Finally, if you try to increase *plié* by forcing the upward bending of the ankle, the arch rolls up and out, thereby (again) weakening or straining the outer ankle ligaments.

Inversion Sprains

An inversion sprain is a stretching or tearing, partial or complete, of one or more of the three ligaments that bind the outer aspect of the ankle. The most common site for this type of injury is the anterior talofibular ligament, the frontmost of the three outer ankle ligaments. A violent turning under of the outside of the foot (forced inversion) is usually the culprit. Such a turning under is even more destructive if at the same time the foot is turned under, the toes are also turned under. You should note that when the foot is *en pointe* there is a certain amount of ligament laxity or instability that predisposes the dancer to this type of strain, unlike in *demi-plié,* when the joint is locked and most stable. Indeed, the very act of pointing the foot makes this type of injury fairly common among dancers, especially if you sickle or roll out. The unavoidable slips or turns that occur place an unusual degree of strain on this vulnerable joint and cause the immobilizing stretching or tearing of the ligaments that bind it. Recurrent injury to the outer ankle ligaments may in fact cause a permanently weakened joint that "gives" without warning. If this is the case, you should always take special care with such steps as *emboité* or *saut de basque.*

Diagnosis

The mechanism of injury—a violent, forcible rolling under of the outer aspect of the foot, so often the result of a "bad landing"— causes a partial or total displacement of the talus (ankle bone), depending on whether the ligaments are simply stretched, or worse, torn. When you sustain an inversion sprain, you usually feel the pain immediately, and it often radiates from the point of injury. Occasionally you even notice a "popping" sensation. In severe sprains of the ankle the leg muscles that move the joint go into spasm. At first you find that you are able to bear *some* weight, but with difficulty, and walk with a limp. Soon, however, you will find it impossible to bear weight on the joint, and the pain becomes rather acute.

Probe lightly with your fingers around the outside of the ankle joint. If a specific point of pain is discernable just in front of the outer ankle bone (lateral malleolus), then your anterior talofibular ligament is involved; you have sustained a "one-ligament" sprain. If sharp pain is elicited directly beneath the lateral malleolus also, then it is likely that you have stretched the calcaneo-fibular ligament as well, thus a "two-ligament" sprain.

Once you have determined the anatomical location of the sprain, it is good to determine the degree of the injury. A first degree sprain is characterized by mild swelling and tenderness. By following the prescribed treatment below, you may expect to return to class in four or five days. You may work at the *barre,* however, if the pain is not disabling. With second degree sprains, in addition to the tenderness and swelling, you find that it is difficult to move the ankle up and down. You should not consider returning to class or *barre* in less than seven days and might even have to stay out for as many as ten to twelve. A third degree sprain produces rapid swelling accompanied by rather intense pain. There is no movement at the ankle, and a black and blue bruise usually develops. You should not plan any activity for up to three weeks if you have sustained a third degree ankle sprain; consult your physician.

Treatment

During the acute stage, or for as long as the ankle joint remains unstable, you should keep it strapped with tape or supported with an elastic ankle brace. For minor, first degree ankle sprains this simple "reminder" strapping may suffice. Remember, *do not tape a badly swollen ankle immediately after injury.* Use an Ace elastic bandage until the swelling goes down.

1. Prepare the area around the ankle and under the heel by painting with benzoin or spraying with pretape such as Tuf-Skin.
2. Take a strip of 1- or 1½-inch cloth tape, anchoring it first just under the medial malleolus (*inner* ankle bone), pulling it under

the heel, then up the outside of the ankle to a point some two inches above the lateral malleolus (*outer* ankle bone).

3. Apply a second strip of tape in the same manner, but overlapping by one-half.

4. Secure the upper ends with two strips of two-inch tape that are wrapped circumferentially around the leg above the ankle bones. Wear an elastic ankle brace over this strapping for additional support.

For a more severe inversion sprain you will want to use this traditional and more supportive method of ankle strapping. It is modified here for ease of application. Use 1- or 1½-inch cloth tape.

1. Prepare the skin by painting with benzoin or spraying with pretape such as Tuf-Skin.

2. Cut out a U-shaped pad from quarter-inch adhesive-backed felt and place it directly below the outer ankle bone, with the wings enveloping it.

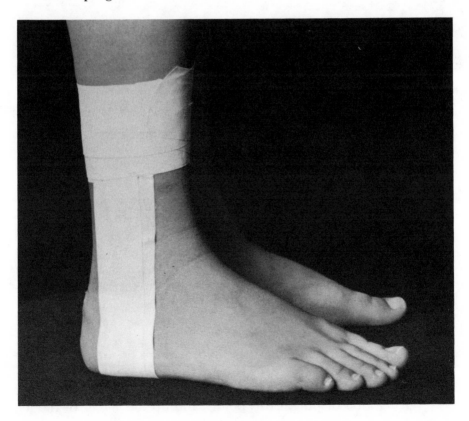

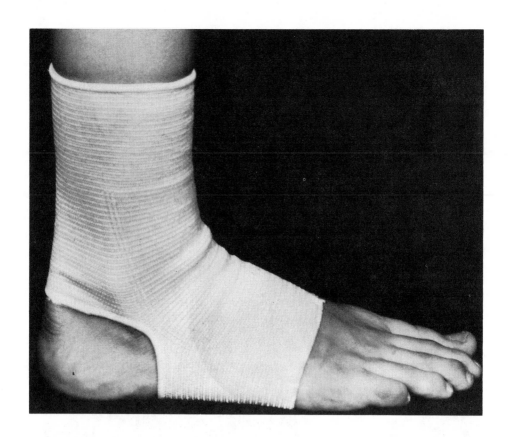

3. Next, secure two anchor strips of 1½- or 2-inch cloth tape, approximately three to four inches above the ankle bones, bringing them circumferentially around the leg (no pressure is applied), front to back.

4. Apply two anchor strips of cloth tape, as above, just in front of the base of the fifth metatarsal, around the foot, sole to top.

5. Place a two by two-inch gauze pad which you have saturated with Vaseline just above the heel, and another two by two-inch pad on top of the foot just below the ankle. These will prevent blisters or cutting from the tape at these vulnerable points.

For the remainder of this strapping the foot should be kept at a right angle."

6. Begin your first *stirrup* at the anchor strap at the back of the ankle on the *inside*. Secure the upper end and run the tape down the leg, behind the *inner* ankle bone, under and around the heel (giving a bit of pull at this point), and up the *outside* of the leg

SIMPLE ANKLE STRAPPING

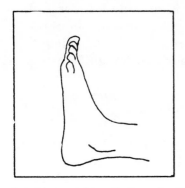

Foot is held at a right angle throughout this taping procedure.

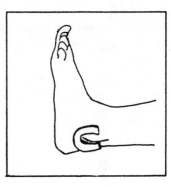

U-shaped adhesive felt pad in position around outer ankle bone.

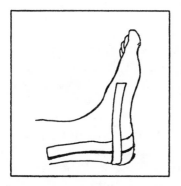

Position of stirrup and horseshoe straps.

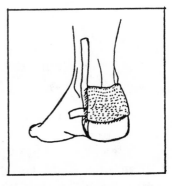

Vaseline-impregnated gauze pad covers Achilles tendon; two stirrups and two horseshoes straps in position.

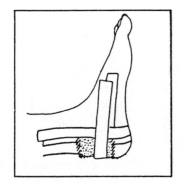

Vaseline-impregnated gauze pad protects Achilles tendon.

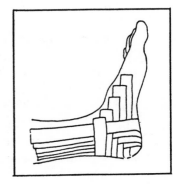

Strapping in place.

behind the outer ankle bone, securing to the anchor strip.

7. Apply a second anchor strip which overlaps the first by one-half. *Note:* The tape does not encircle the leg exactly, but angles somewhat to conform to its shape.

8. Now place a *horseshoe* strap around the lower aspect of the heel, attaching it to the anchor strip that encircles the foot. (The ends of the horseshoe strap should be brought around simultaneously.) *Note:* The horseshoe straps angle down slightly toward the sole of the foot.

9. Repeat this combination of stirrup-anchor-horseshoe for two or three more times until the outer ankle bone is completely enveloped in tape.

10. Next, using succeeding anchor strips, fill in the remainder of the lower leg *down* to the uppermost horseshoe.

11. The arch of the foot is now filled in, beginning closest to the toes and working back with strips of tape two inches wide.

12. Heel locks may be applied to stabilize the calcaneus. Starting at the top-front of the ankle, bring a strip of 1½-inch tape around the ankle, *inside to out*, then *down* the outside of the heel, under and across the foot, and up the inside, to the starting point. Now apply one or two more strips of tape in this manner, each one overlapping the former by approximately two-thirds.

After seventy-two hours you should commence a regimen of ice and stretching. Massage the ankle with an ice pack or solid piece of ice you have molded in a styrofoam cup. (Some dancers prefer using a bucket of ice-water slush.) Numbing should occur in ten to fifteen minutes. Now, stretch the ankle passively by putting it through its full range of motion: rotate clockwise, then counterclockwise, raise and point the foot, and so on. After you have stretched the ankle, move around on it until it becomes just a *little* sore. *Note:* Moving around on it does not mean dancing or jumping rope; simply walk around as best you can until you notice mild discomfort. Ice the ankle a second time until it becomes numb, then repeat the stretching and movement. Ice one final time for ten minutes or so. Thus you have ice-to-movement-to-ice-to-movement-to-ice. Retape the ankle. This routine will take some forty-five minutes to an hour daily, but you should not fail to do it; the healing process is greatly enhanced, and you will get back to class much sooner. Continue ice-stretching-movement until you can move about freely, without pain and without the tape.

At this point you will want to change your daily routine from one of ice and limited movement to one of strengthening. The *simplest* way to accomplish this is by following this regimen at least three times daily for three to five weeks. Remember, it may be seven to twelve weeks before you completely recover from a *bad* sprain, one that involves badly stretched or torn ligaments, so be patient. Do not rush your treatment or return to class too soon. The chances of reinjury are much too great to risk it.

1. Sit on the floor in front of a desk or the wall and push your injured foot against it as hard as you can, holding for ten to twelve seconds. Repeat four more times.
2. Sit in a chair at a heavy table or desk and push the *outside* of the foot against one of the four legs as hard as you can, holding for ten to twelve seconds. Repeat four more times.
3. While still seated, push the *inside* of the foot against one of the legs as hard as you can, holding for ten to twelve seconds. Repeat four more times.
4. Finally, *raise* your foot against resistance—you can attempt to raise an easy chair, for instance—pulling as hard as you can, holding for ten to twelve seconds. Repeat four more times.

Periodically try this simple "ankle balance test" to determine if the ankle has mended well enough to support your weight during light activity. Get a brick or a thick book, 2½ to 3 inches high, and stand on it with the injured ankle. If you are able to maintain your balance and not fall off, then you're all ready to resume classes. If you cannot keep your balance, then go back to your rehabilitation exercises and keep the ankle taped or supported with an elastic ankle brace. *Note:* You may want to continue using the elastic ankle brace for an extended period just as a *reminder* of the weak ankle.

Eversion Sprains

Eversion sprains occur much less commonly than do inversion sprains of the ankle. However, on certain unfortunate occasions, the dancer will twist under the inner arch in a forceful manner, frequently the result of a "bad landing" or in a *fouetté* or a rapid turn when she is *en pointe*, with the resulting stretching or tearing of the deltoid ligament. Poor balance or general fatigue predisposes to both types of sprain. Among modern dancers eversion sprains can result from any of the rising movements that use the inner arch of the foot. Whatever the mechanism of the injury, however, the condition is quite serious and may lead to prolonged weakness of the ankle and pain in the longitudinal arch. Treatment and rehabilitation are basically the same as for inversion sprains except that you should begin a program of exercises to strengthen the intrinsic muscles of the foot, especially those that support the long arch. Extra *tendus* are especially beneficial. In addition to the taping procedure described above for inversion sprains, you should attach a varus pad to the inside of the heel.

VARUS PAD

1. Prepare the skin by painting with benzoin or spraying with pre-tape such as Tuf-Skin.
2. Trace your heel on a piece of quarter- to half-inch adhesive-backed felt for a length of approximately three to four inches, depending on the size of your foot. Cut out the pattern.
3. Next, cut the heel pad in half and reserve the half that lies under the *inner* side of your heel. Bevel on all sides and attach to the skin under the heel.
4. Tape the ankle securely, as described above for inversion sprains.

The period of healing for an eversion sprain will be somewhat longer than that for an inversion sprain, so do not rush the process. Follow the regimen for rehabilitation and strengthening, and keep the ankle secure at all times. Take special care not to reinjure it.

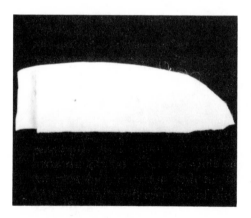
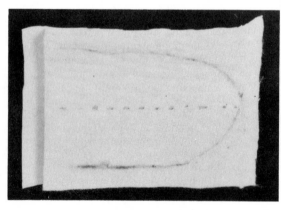

2

Leg

SHINSPLINTS

SHINSPLINTS MAY BE THE SINGLE MOST AGGRAVATING CONDITION THAT troubles dancers on a day to day basis. What actually occurs with shinsplints is a microscopic tearing away of the fibers of certain of the leg muscles from their points of origin around or on the tibia. The result may be any one or combination of the following: inflammation of the muscle itself, with swelling; inflammation of the tendons of the tibialis anterior or posterior muscles which insert into the sole of the foot; or inflammation of the membranous covering of the bone at the points of origin of the affected muscles.

Shinsplints occur most commonly after hard workouts on hard, unresilient floors; from intensive jumpings or leaps; or simply after a prolonged layoff when you do not stretch or warm up properly. This condition is also quite common in young dancers who are learning fifth position or in any dancer with flat or pronated feet, or who sickles or rolls over en pointe.

There are three general categories which may be applicable; the first two of which are true shinsplints, the third, a condition which is much more serious, but in its early stages is often confused with shinsplints. They are: *anterior tibial shinsplints,* with pain occurring along the crest or ridge of the tibia (shinbone); *posterior tibial shinsplints,* with pain occurring deep within the inner side of the calf

147

MUSCLES AT THE ANTERIOR (FRONT) ASPECT OF THE LEG
(after Barcsay's *Anatomy*)

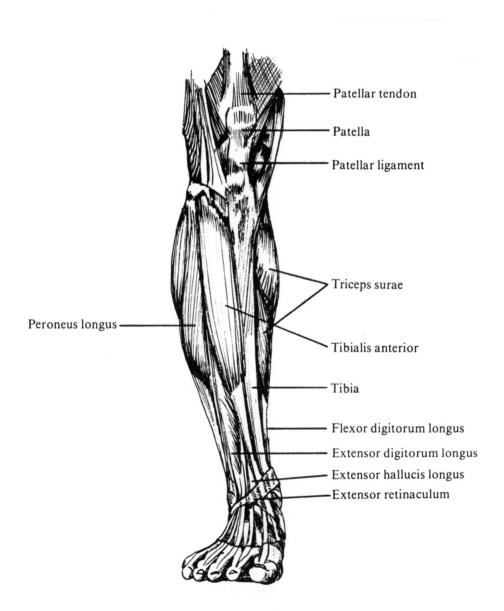

Patellar tendon

Patella

Patellar ligament

Triceps surae

Peroneus longus

Tibialis anterior

Tibia

Flexor digitorum longus

Extensor digitorum longus

Extensor hallucis longus

Extensor retinaculum

POSTERIOR (BACK) VIEW OF LEFT LEG
SHOWING TIBIALIS POSTERIOR MUSCLE

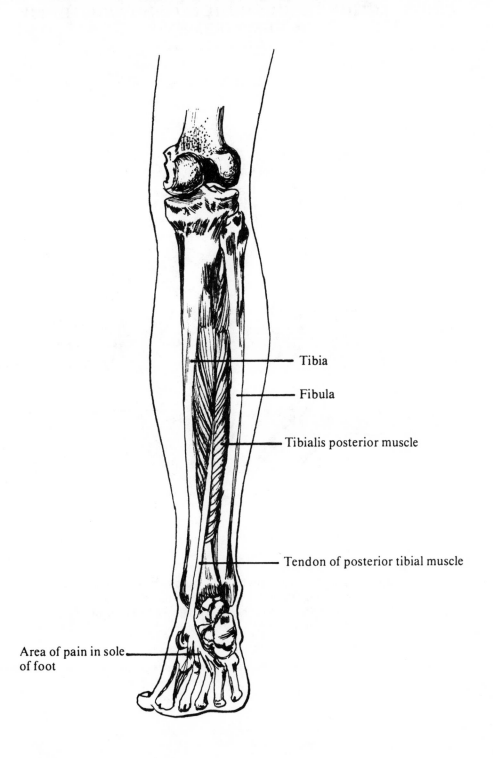

Tibia

Fibula

Tibialis posterior muscle

Tendon of posterior tibial muscle

Area of pain in sole
of foot

CROSS SECTION THROUGH THE LEG SHOWING THE MUSCLE COMPARTMENTS

(after Grant's *Atlas*)

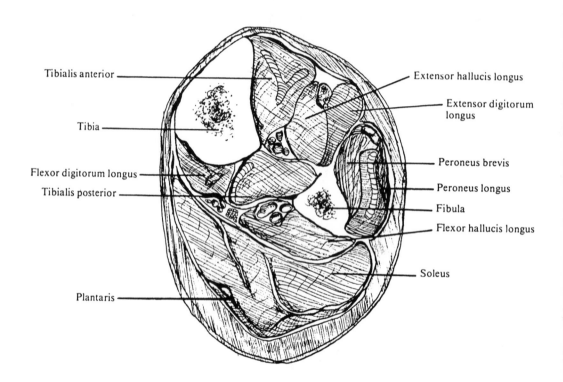

Tibialis anterior

Tibia

Flexor digitorum longus

Tibialis posterior

Plantaris

Extensor hallucis longus

Extensor digitorum longus

Peroneus brevis

Peroneus longus

Fibula

Flexor hallucis longus

Soleus

The muscles in the anterior compartment are seen in this diagram to the right of the tibia: the tibialis anterior, extensor hallucis longus, and extensor digitorum longus.

between the gastrocnemius and tibia; and *anterior compartment syndrome,* an extremely serious condition affecting all the muscles in the anterior compartment which expand in size too great for the area anatomically provided, with the result that circulation and nerve supply are restricted. In the first two categories there is much you can do yourself to deal with the pain and in alleviating the predisposing factors; in the third, anterior compartment syndrome, surgical decompression of the area may be required to render the area pain free.

Diagnosis

You probably already know the symptoms of shinsplints all too well, but with *anterior tibial shinsplints* there is a sharp shooting pain along the lower front aspect of the leg following a course that parallels the crest of the tibia or lies just to the side of it. Pressing along this aspect of the bone, you are often able to find one particularly painful point. Also, the pain commonly begins about three inches above the ankle and extends up the leg for another two to four inches or more. With *posterior tibial shinsplints* a duller but more persistent pain is experienced deep in the muscle area between the border of the calf muscle and the shinbone. This pain may extend down to and behind the inner ankle bone and usually comes on two or three hours *after* class has ended. If you point your toes down and roll the arch upward, the pain becomes more sensitive to the touch. With both anterior and posterior tibial shinsplints you frequently are able to locate an extremely painful area at the high point of the arch of the foot. Finally, with *anterior compartment syndrome* a burning sensation is felt on the *outside* of the leg and is often accompanied by tingling or numbness and a marked loss of strength in the leg. It is difficult for you to raise the front of the foot, and numbness may be present. The pain with anterior compartment syndrome increases with activity as the leg muscles swell with blood. If what you had formerly suspected to be chronic shinsplints seems now to resemble a compartment syndrome instead, you should consult an orthopedist immediately. Permanent damage may occur if the condition is allowed to persist.

Before proceeding, let us mention briefly a condition that, while not so common among dancers, does occasionally occur, *tibial stress fracture.* You in fact may confuse a tibial stress fracture with persistent shinsplints. Basically, the predisposing factors for a tibial stress fracture are the same as for shinsplints, but the pain that finally results is located about a quarter to a third of the way down the tibia

151

ANTERIOR TIBIAL SHINSPLINTS AND ANTERIOR COMPARTMENT SYNDROME

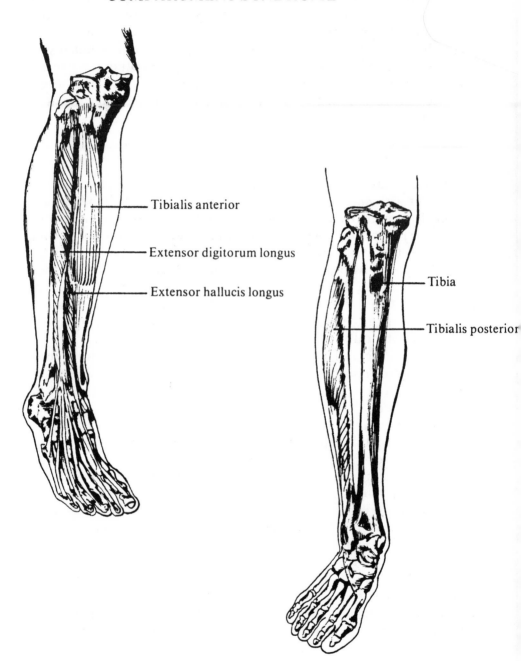

Tibialis anterior

Extensor digitorum longus

Extensor hallucis longus

Tibia

Tibialis posterior

POSTERIOR TIBIAL SHINSPLINTS

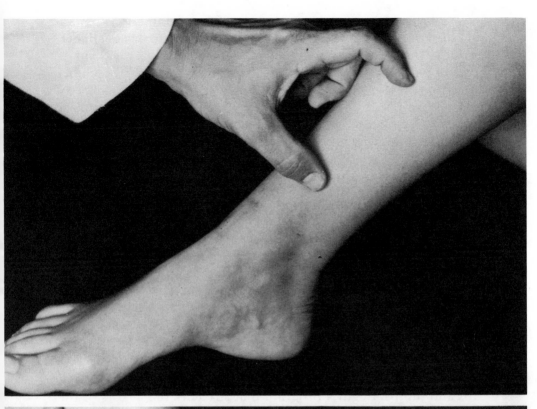

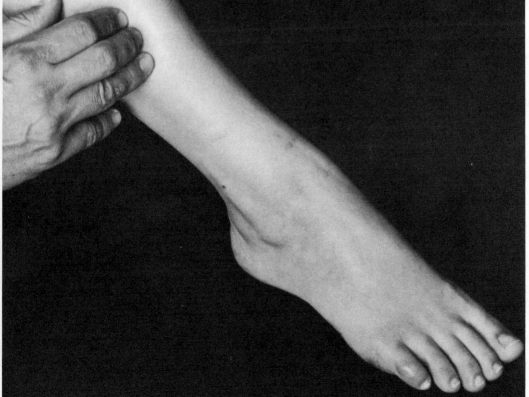

from the knee joint, not on the lower inner side (as in certain athletic activities). In some cases a hard bony mass may be felt at the point of intensest pain, but do not confuse it with the tuberosity of the tibia (see section on Osgood-Schlatter's disease)—a perfectly normal bony eminence on the front, upper shin—with an abnormal bony mass secondary to a tibial stress fracture. The discomfort you feel is much more severe with a stress fracture than with shinsplints and will not respond well, if at all, to standard modalities of treatment as described below. If you even suspect that you might have a tibial stress fracture, you should not hesitate to consult an orthopedist as soon as possible. He can confirm or allay your suspicions with a bone scan.

Treatment

Rest is extremely important in dealing with shinsplints, so get as much as you possibly can. After class ice the area for at least twenty minutes, and, if you have time, apply moist heat to the shin before class. Take three or four aspirin every four hours for three days, two every six hours thereafter as needed. Wear half-inch heel lifts in your street shoes. You should avoid pointe work altogether because it aggravates the condition and makes the pain more intense. Avoid leaps and jumps. Begin a program that stretches the flexors of the foot (the muscles that point the toes). Warm-up should always include *relevé* and *demi-plié*.

For a simple case of shinsplints that is more aggravating than painful try this basic strapping. Many dancers have found that i provides the degree of relief they need.

1. Press along the painful area of the shin and locate the exact point where the pain is most severe. You should mark this point with a felt-tipped pen.
2. Shave away any hair in the area to be taped and prepare the skin by painting with benzoin or spraying with pretape such as Tuf-Skin.
3. Flex (bend) the leg and keep it flexed while the tape is being applied.
4. *Optional.* Cut out an oval from sixteenth-inch adhesive-backed felt and bevel on all sides. Attach it to the point that you have marked on the shin.
5. Beginning approximately one inch *below* the pad, or below the point of severest pain if you are not using a pad, apply four or five strips of 1- or 1½-inch cloth adhesive tape, each one overlap-

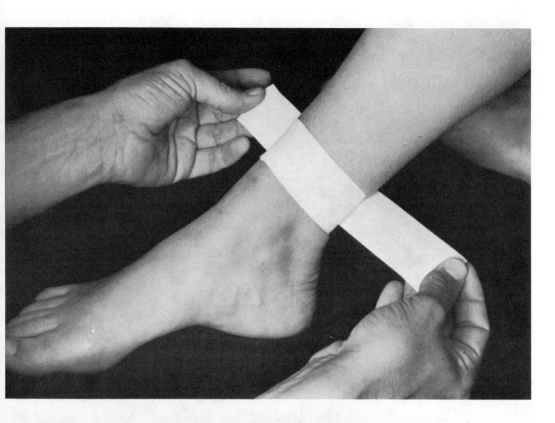

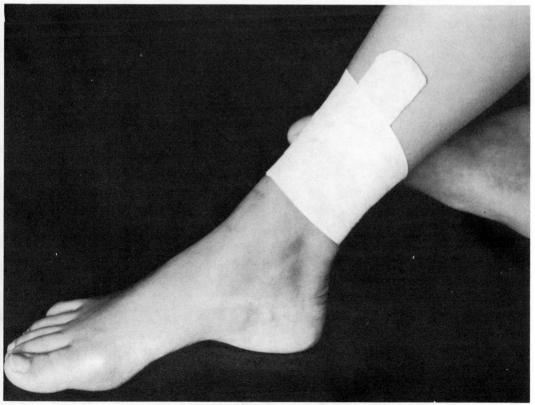

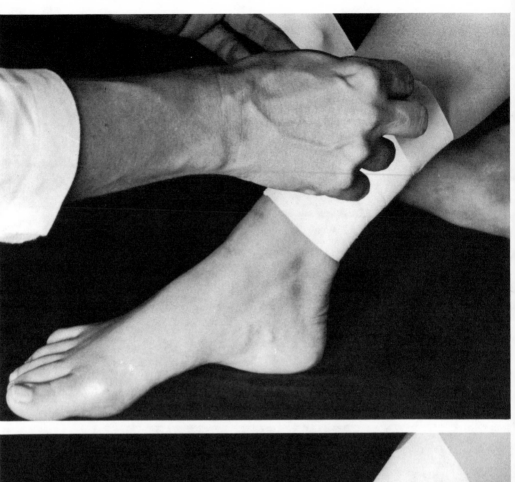

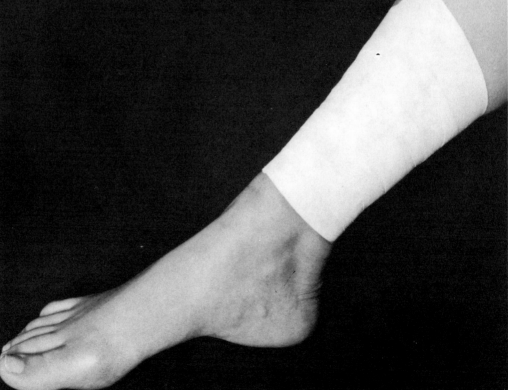

ping the former by one-half. These strips should extend an inch or so beyond the padding (or point of pain). Remember, simply lay the tape around the leg, front to back; no pressure should be applied. If it is too tight, then you must not continue class until you have loosened it.

You may keep the leg taped in this fashion for as long as necessary, but it is good to begin a regimen of exercises that will stretch the tibialis muscles. While at rest, watching TV, sitting in class, or wherever, do foot circles with the foot extended (pointed), twenty-five in a clockwise direction, then twenty-five in a counterclockwise direction. Do these as often as you are able. Alternate with this routine: point your foot forcibly and hold for a count of ten (one thousand and one, one thousand and two, and so on); next point the foot *in* and hold for a count of ten; finally, forcibly pull the foot toward your head as far as possible and hold for a count of ten. Try to do five repetitions.

For a more chronic or persistent case of shinsplints you should attach a support pad to the arch of the foot as well as tape the leg. This is rather easy to do.

1. Paint the skin with benzoin or spray with pretape such as Tuf-Skin.
2. Cut a half-moon shaped piece from quarter- or three-eighths-inch felt, approximately 3 to 3½ inches long and 2½ inches wide at the center. Bevel on all sides.
3. Strap this pad in place with strips of 1- or 1½-inch cloth tape laid around the sole from bottom to top, where the ends cross. This tape should not be applied with pressure but merely laid around. The strapping should feel snug and supportive. (See section on "Metatarsalgia.")

For a more serious case of shinsplints you must pad the arch in the manner described above and apply an X-type strapping to the shin.

1. Shave the leg from ankle to knee and paint with benzoin or spray with pretape.
2. Cut strips of 1½- or 2-inch cloth adhesive tape approximately five to six inches long. Starting at a point about an inch *below* where the shinsplint pain begins, apply your strips in a criss-cross or X-fashion, each succeeding pair overlapping the former by one-half, right up the leg to a point just below the knee. *Note:* You

157

should attach these strips with a certain amount of pull, so anchor the lower attached end with your thumb and pull the strip upward before you lay it down and attach to the skin.

3. You may anchor the bottom and top ends with two- or three-inch circumferential taping if you like, two layers each.

Regardless of the taping technique you find most useful, it is still good to use an eighth- or three-eighths-inch heel lift in your street shoes. You might also try an eighth-inch lift in your point shoes as well. To prevent shinsplints in the future you should work hard to stretch the tibialis anterior and posterior, and if the calf muscle is tight (it *probably* is), begin stretching it as well.

PERONEAL TENDINITIS

The peroneus longus and brevis muscles, which arise on the outer aspect of the leg between the tibia and fibula, raise the outer border of the foot and assist in pointing it. Dancers who roll in in an effort to improve turnout or those who sickle predispose themselves to inflammation of the tendons of these muscles. And when the peroneal tendons become inflamed (occasionally even the result of fatigue that is brought on by poor technique) such movements as *ronde de jambe* become quite painful and difficult to execute.

Diagnosis

You will notice a particularly painful point just behind or under the outer ankle bone. It often extends up the leg for two or three inches. The outer aspect of the leg aches and fatigues easily. Typically there is swelling around the outer ankle bone which gives it a "puffy" appearance. Indeed the ankle itself feels weak. You notice that pain increases significantly *after* rather than during class. Any position that raises you on your toes—*relevé*, for instance—causes a deep-seated aching pain; you fatigue rather easily in class. Also, if you are rolling in to improve turnout, the pain usually becomes more acute. If the condition is left unattended, pain under the cuboid bone (outer side of the foot) may develop as well, where the peroneus longus passes beneath it.

Treatment

Treatment consists of mild support for the peroneal tendons and the area around the mid-foot beneath the cuboid. Initially, however,

MEDIAL (INNER) VIEW OF LEG MUSCLES
(after Barscay's *Anatomy*)

LATERAL (OUTER)
VIEW OF LEG MUSCLES
(after Barscay's *Anatomy*)

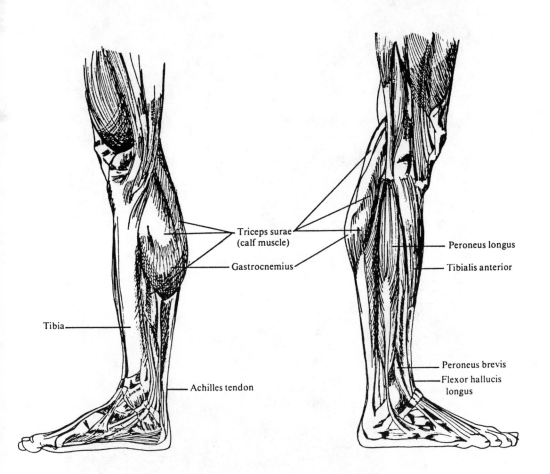

Triceps surae
(calf muscle)

Gastrocnemius

Tibia

Achilles tendon

Peroneus longus

Tibialis anterior

Peroneus brevis

Flexor hallucis
longus

you can deal with the inflammation by icing the outer aspect of the leg for a period of fifteen to twenty minutes, three times daily. Take aspirin, three or four every four hours for the first three days, two every four hours thereafter as needed. Try strapping the leg and padding the foot in this fashion.

1. Prepare the skin by painting with benzoin or spraying with pre-tape such as Tuf-Skin.
2. Flex the leg and keep it flexed while the tape is being applied. Using strips of 1- or 1½-inch cloth tape, begin at the ankle bone

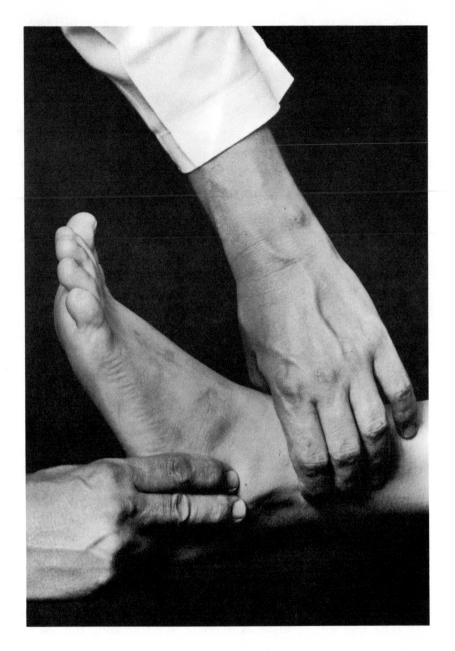

or slightly above and wrap around four or five strips. Each strip should overlap the former by one-half. Remember, these strips should be brought around the sides of the leg, back to front, with no tension whatsoever. They cross *over* the shin bone.

3. Cut a rectangular pad from eighth- or quarter-inch adhesive-backed felt and round the corners and bevel on all sides. The pad

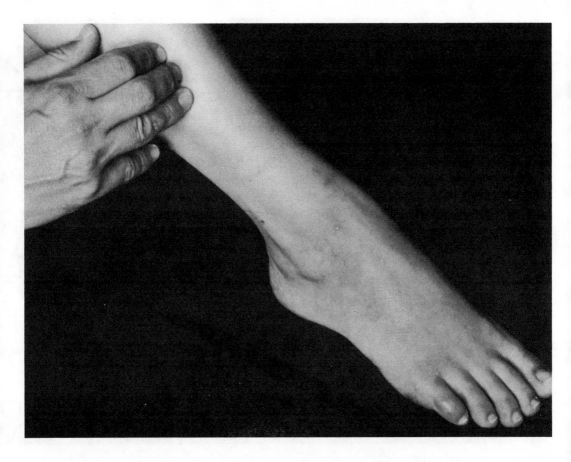

should be large enough to extend from the center of the foot, under the cuboid, to a point just above the outer edge. (The outer aspect of this pad should be double- or triple-beveled; see section on "Subluxed Cuboid.")
4. Strap the cuboid pad in place with 1- or 1½-inch cloth tape.

Place quarter- or three-eighths-inch felt heel lifts in your street shoes, and eighth-inch felt lifts in your pointe shoes. Symptomatic improvement should come on fairly rapidly if you allow yourself a reasonable amount of rest and apply the strapping and padding described—usually three or four days. You may want to continue with the strapping for several weeks, however, in order not to over-strain the weakened peroneals. As soon as you are able, certainly within the first week of recovery, ask your teacher to describe a regimen of exercises that stretch and strengthen the peroneals. Extra *battements tendus* in class strengthen the foot muscles which support the cuboid.

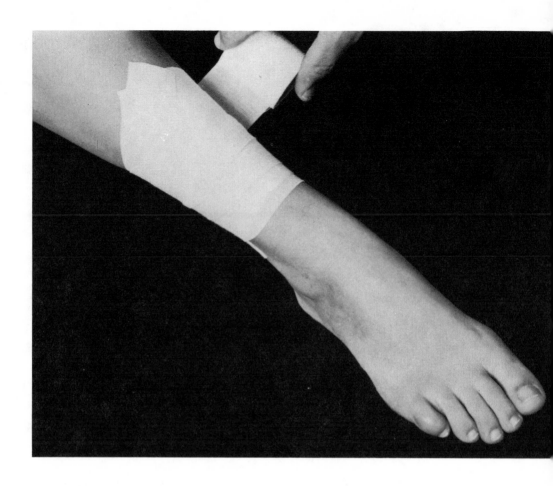

STRAINED CALF MUSCLE

A strained or pulled calf muscle is quite common among dancers and is usually the result of insufficient warm-up, general fatigue, or rehearsing on hard, unresilient floors. The most common sight of injury is at the point where the muscle becomes tendinous (which, incidentally, is the point where *all muscles are* most vulnerable). Improper technique—forcing turnout, rolling or sickling—certainly predisposes you to this sort of injury. The pain that results runs horizontally *across* the calf at the point where the calf muscle joins the Achilles tendon. *Note:* The pain from a pulled plantaris muscle runs *up and down* leg rather than across it.

Treatment

The best treatment for a pulled calf muscle is rest. Take aspirin,

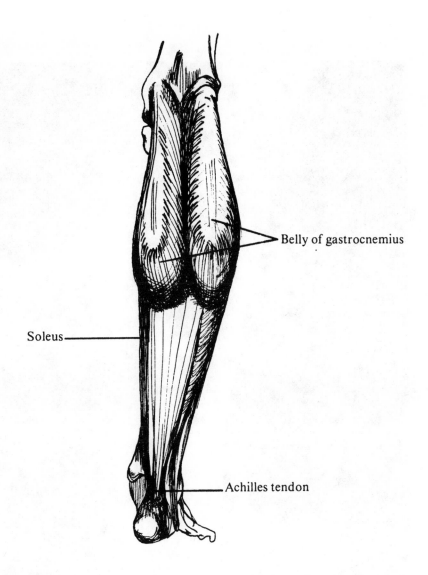

Belly of gastrocnemius

Soleus

Achilles tendon

three every four hours for three days, two every six hours thereafter as needed, to control the inflammation. Icing the calf at the point of injury—ten minutes on, ten minutes off, for a half hour—will also help reduce the inflammation and any swelling that might have developed. After three days you will find that moist heat and light massage will prove beneficial. Heel lifts, three-eighths- or half-inch felt or sponge rubber, will reduce the "pull" on the muscle. Finally, wrap the muscle circumferentially with a two-inch Ace bandage or

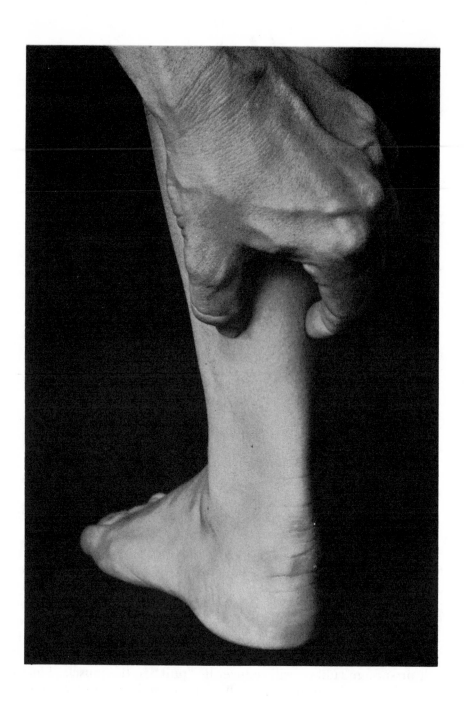

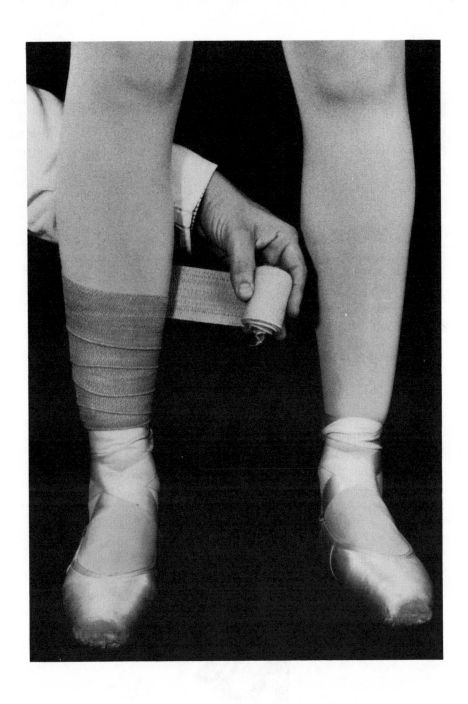

elastic "J-wrap" from the ankle to a point just below the knee, with each succeeding turn overlapping the former by one-half to two-thirds. This will go far to reduce the strain on the muscle as it heals.

PULLED SOLEUS MUSCLE

The soleus muscle is broad and flat and lies deep within the calf against the leg bone. At its lower aspect it becomes common with the gastrocnemius. Together these muscles raise the heel to point the foot. The soleus is especially prone to overuse and will tighten up and get quite sore if you do not stretch and warm up enough. A dull, persistent aching pain occurs approximately midway down the calf. It feels "deep" rather than superficial. Squeezing the muscle at this point usually produces a rather sharp pain.

DEEP MUSCLES OF THE LEG
(Gastronemius has been removed)
(after Barcsay's *Anatomy*)

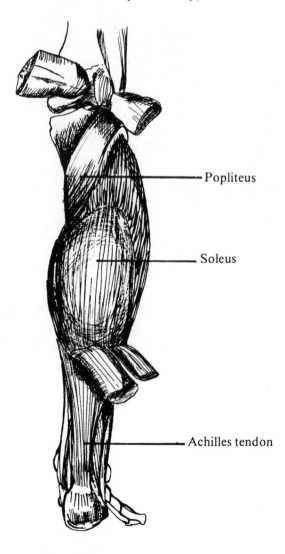

Popliteus

Soleus

Achilles tendon

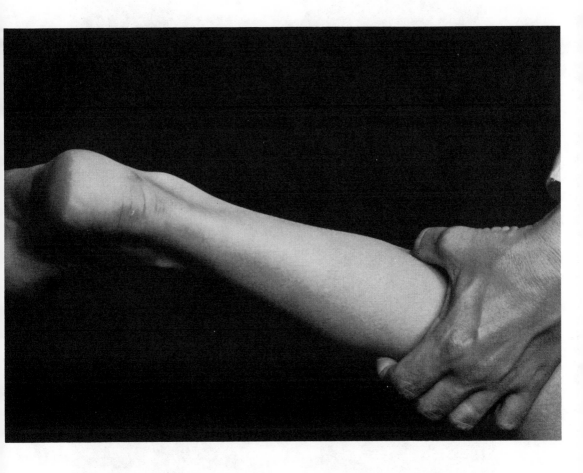

Treatment

To control the swelling and inflammation, take three or four aspirin every four hours for up to three days, two aspirin every six hours
thereafter as needed. A cold towel applied to the area or ice massage

167

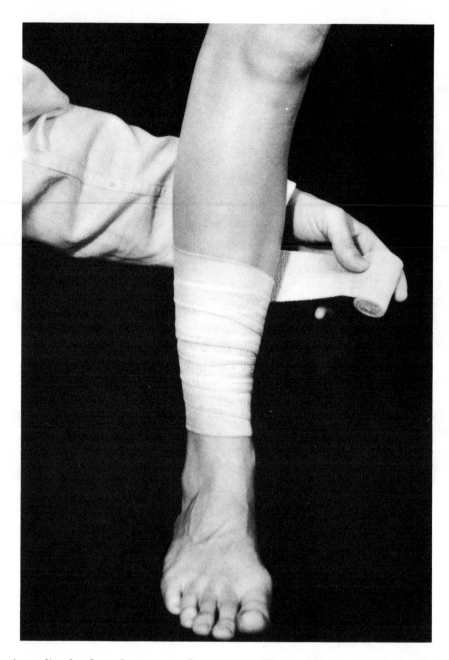

immediately after class or performance will provide a degree of relief. You may support the calf muscle by wrapping it with an Ace bandage from just above the ankle bones to a point just below the knee; each turn of the bandage overlaps the former by one-half. You may also wear a three-eighths or half-inch heel lift in the shoe of the affected leg to take some of the strain off the muscle. After three days begin applying moist heat at night and before class. *Note:* If the calf muscle is especially tight (which it most likely is) you should begin a regimen of stretching exercises. Ask your teacher or consult a local fitness studio for advice as to which exercise might best be suited to your needs. Also, see the section on "Achilles Tendinitis."

TORN PLANTARIS MUSCLE

The plantaris muscle is a small but extremely long vestigial muscle about the size of a pencil that is located deep in the upper aspect of the leg; its tendon runs down the inner side of the calf. (Cats use the

THE PLANTARIS MUSCLE

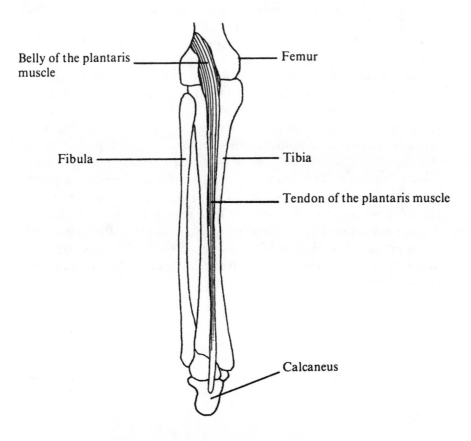

Belly of the plantaris muscle

Femur

Fibula

Tibia

Tendon of the plantaris muscle

Calcaneus

The plantaris muscle lies deep within the leg, along the shaft of the tibia.

plantaris to bare their claws, but it is of little use to dancers—except when they bare their claws!) Because of its size and location this muscle is prone to rupture and tearing, although the injury is much more common in older dancers than younger. The pain that results is often confused with a strain or pulling of the gastrocnemius.

Diagnosis

You usually hear a snap and experience what seems to be a violent blow to the back side of the calf. There is extreme pain and swelling. You find it difficult to bear weight on your heel and tend to walk on the ball of your foot. The pain characteristically runs *up and down* the calf, not across it, as with a strained calf muscle.

Treatment

You should ice the area *immediately,* for twenty to thirty minutes. Repeat the icing three or four times a day for three days. Thereafter you should change over to heat, preferably a hydrocollator pad or whirlpool, if available. Use a three-eighths- or half-inch heel lift of felt or sponge rubber in all of your shoes. Further relief is obtained by applying an Ace bandage to the calf, starting just above the ankle bone and wrapping it up to a point just below the knee, each succeeding turn overlapping the former by one-half to two-thirds. Some dancers have found that the application of a Low Dye strap to the foot also affords a degree of relief (see section on "Plantar Fasciitis"). While all of these measures will facilitate the healing process, do not expect a torn plantaris to improve significantly in less than ten days to two or three weeks; so take it easy. You will only lose time if you get back to the *barre* too soon. *Note:* Because the plantaris has no significant function in humans, its absence, the result of tearing or rupture, is seldom noticed. Surgical repair, therefore, is not a consideration.

3

Knee

INJURIES OF THE KNEE JOINT: CARTILAGE AND LIGAMENTS

THE KNEE JOINT IS THE STRONGEST AND ONE OF THE MOST COMPLEX joints in the body. It is made up of the articulation of the femur (thigh bone) and tibia (leg bone). Its strength comes principally from the ligaments that hold these two bones together. Attached to the head, or top, of the tibia are the *medial* (inner) and *lateral* (outer) *menisci,* which are made up of cartilaginous tissue. These menisci serve to deepen the joint and cushion it from shock. Within the joint and between the menisci are the internal knee ligaments, the *anterior* (front) and *posterior* (back) *cruciate ligaments.* To the front and sides of the knee joint are the *medial* and *lateral collateral ligaments.* The collateral ligaments allow the flexing (bending) action of the joint and limit somewhat any side to side motion. Dancers will notice, however, that they have developed to some extent the ability to rotate the knee joint in a *ronds de jambe.*

There are some basic anatomical considerations of interest to the dancer. The internal and collateral ligaments of the knee are held tight when the knee is extended (straight). However, when the knee is partially flexed (bent), the internal cruciate and lateral collateral ligaments are loose; only the medial collateral ligament remains tight. Thus, the straight or extended knee joint is more stable than the flexed knee joint and is less prone to sudden injury. Finally,

THE KNEE JOINT

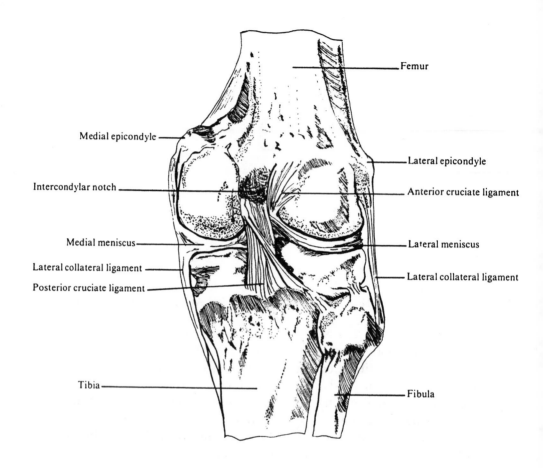

Femur

Medial epicondyle

Lateral epicondyle

Intercondylar notch

Anterior cruciate ligament

Medial meniscus

Lateral meniscus

Lateral collateral ligament

Lateral collateral ligament

Posterior cruciate ligament

Tibia

Fibula

(after Grant's *Atlas*)

because the medial meniscus is attached to the medial collateral ligament, an improper landing from a jump that twists a slightly flexed knee joint stretches or tears the medial collateral ligament and may, as a consequence, also damage the medial meniscus.

The dancer who forces turnout, rolls over *en pointe,* or falls inward when rising from a *plié* is greatly predisposed to knee injury. Rolling over also puts a tremendous strain on both the knee cartilages and ligaments and may eventually lead to tearing or loosening of these structures. Good technique, therefore, is the best preventative. You

INTERNAL STRUCTURE OF THE KNEE JOINT
(after Grant's *Atlas*)

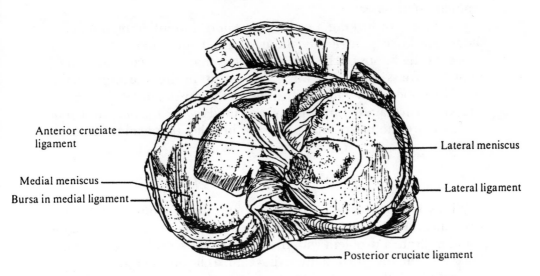

Anterior cruciate ligament

Medial meniscus

Bursa in medial ligament

Lateral meniscus

Lateral ligament

Posterior cruciate ligament

will need to begin a program of stretching of the front of the hip because, as you have probably noticed already, tightness at the front of the hips puts excessive strain on the weight-bearing leg. Only during *grand pliés* and deep *fondus* is the supporting leg significantly flexed at the hip. Tight turnout can and usually will produce injuries of the knee menisci or cartilage. Also, for any serious knee problem you will need to strengthen the adductor muscles of the hip, as they play an extremely important role in stabilizing the pelvis and provide control in holding and improve turnout. Finally, you must also strengthen the inner thigh muscles as well as the entire extensor mechanism.

Aside from faulty technique, however, there is always the chance of a violent twisting movement affecting the knee joint, especially when the foot is firmly planted, or even a twist of the thigh when the knee is locked, either of which could result in cartilage damage. "Screwing the knee" to close in fifth position may also lead to ligament damage, especially with males who have inflexible hips and force turnout from the knees. Shearing tears of the meniscus may also result from "screwing" the knee. And, last but not least, one of the most common predisposing factors to knee injury is the dancer's failure to keep the knees directly over the feet in *pliés*.

Diagnosis

You may suspect some degree of knee injury when there is fluid accumulation, "giving way," or locking of the joint in a partially extended position. In any of the diagnostic tests that follow, always compare both knees.

Giving way or locking, persistent swelling and inflammation, pain along the knee joint itself (about one-half inch above the upper aspect of the knobs of the tibia), a feeling that the knee "goes out of joint," stiffness, especially when you get up in the morning, or the inability to bend the knee fully indicate the possibility of damage to the knee cartilages. Improperly executed *ronds de jambe* and *petit battement* are the most common moves in ballet that lead to cartilage damage.

TEST FOR CARTILAGE DAMAGE

With your foot turned out, extend (straighten) your knee against resistance. A "clicking" sound or pain on the *inside* of the knee joint could indicate a problem with the medial meniscus. Now extend the knee with the foot turned inward. Again, a clicking sound or pain on the *outside* of the knee joint could indicate damage to the lateral meniscus. In either instance moving the kneecap back and forth is likely to produce a "splashing" feeling if there is cartilage damage.

Damage to the medial collateral ligament is on the order of four or five times greater than damage to the lateral collateral ligament. Swelling, which commonly does not appear for thirty minutes or so after a ligament has been damaged, loss or reduction of movement in the joint, pain with leg extension (straightening), pain with rotation of the knee when the joint is partially flexed, or the inability to place your foot flat on the floor (with a consequent tendency for you to walk on your toes) are among the principal symptoms of knee ligament injury.

TEST FOR LIGAMENT DAMAGE

Straightening the leg against resistance will usually produce pain at the site of injury if a ligament is involved. Also direct pressure to the point will also elicit a painful response.

Treatment

If you suspect you have pulled or torn a knee cartilage, it is good to consult an orthopedist immediately for an accurate assessment of the situation. For minor sprains of the knee ligaments, medial or lateral, there is much you can do to assist in the healing process. Complete rest is of utmost importance—as much as you can possibly allow yourself. Ice the knee for a period of twenty minutes, at least three times a day. While icing, the knee should be kept extended (straight) at body level, or slightly elevated. During the session, while your knee is locked, forcibly contract the quadriceps and hold for a few seconds, relax, then repeat. The quadriceps atrophies faster than any other muscle group in the body, so you will want to do what you can to keep the quads in tone. Take aspirin for the inflammation, three or four every four hours for the first seventy-two hours, two every four hours thereafter as needed. Support the knee with

TESTING FOR STRAINED KNEE LIGAMENTS

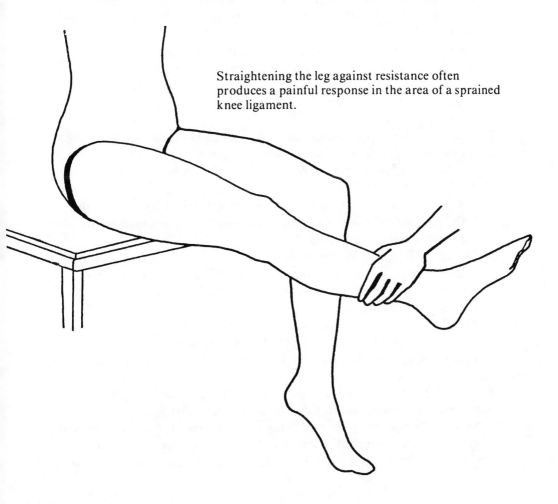

Straightening the leg against resistance often produces a painful response in the area of a sprained knee ligament.

an elastic knee brace or an Ace bandage when you must be up and about, but keep it elevated as much as possible. You may also want to strap the injured knee for additional stability, but, as a dancer, you should strap only the weak side; full knee taping limits the joint motion beyond the point you are able to dance on it. Furthermore, if strapping the one side only does not provide the necessary stability on a temporary basis, you should not be dancing. *See an orthopedist!*

1. Prepare the knee and the area above and below it by shaving, if necessary, and painting with benzoin or spraying with pretape such Tuf-Skin.
2. Place a book under the heel so that the knee is flexed at a fifteen to twenty degree angle.
3. Place two circumferential anchor straps of two- or three-inch cloth tape just *below* the midpoint of the thigh and two just *above* the midpoint of the calf. Do not apply these straps with pressure but simply wrap them around.
4. Using two-inch *elastic* tape, apply a strip to the anchor strap below the knee, *on the outside,* and pull it around, up, and diagonally toward the anchor strap on the thigh (this course roughly follows the line of the femur, or thigh bone), where it is attached with just a little pressure and pull.
5. The second strip of elastic tape also commences below the knee, *on the inside* however, and is pulled diagonally over the inside of the knee and attached to the outside of the thigh.
6. Repeat this pattern with three more succeeding strips of elastic tape, each one overlapping the former by approximately one-half, so that you form an "X" with eight intersecting strips of tape, four from each direction.
7. Next, anchor the lower end of the "X" with strips of 1½-inch adhesive tape, beginning just below the knee, and moving toward the ankle until you have reached the anchor strap around the upper calf; again, each layer overlaps the former by one-half.
8. Finally, anchor the upper end of the "X" with strips of 1½-inch adhesive tape, moving upward from the knee toward the hip, ending at the circumferential strap around the lower thigh.

This strapping provides temporary stabilization only. A seriously damaged knee must be attended by an orthopedist.

As soon as you are able you must begin to recondition the quadriceps with strengthening exercises. Ask your teacher or trainer for advice as to the proper ones for your particular circumstances. Re-

PROTECTIVE STRAPPING FOR INJURED KNEE LIGAMENTS AND CARTILAGE

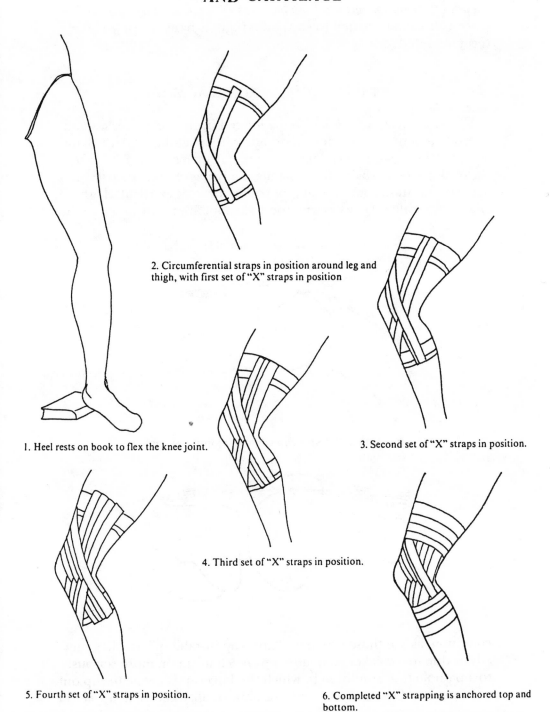

1. Heel rests on book to flex the knee joint.

2. Circumferential straps in position around leg and thigh, with first set of "X" straps in position

3. Second set of "X" straps in position.

4. Third set of "X" straps in position.

5. Fourth set of "X" straps in position.

6. Completed "X" strapping is anchored top and bottom.

member, however, that the great danger in follow-up is beginning your reconditioning program before the knee has healed. *You must not bend the joint forcibly until you have passed the acute stage of the injury.* Once you have returned to class on a regular basis, extra *tendus* are recommended.

PATELLA CHONDROMALACIA

The kneecap is a sesamoid bone lodged in the belly of the quadriceps ligament. It provides the femur with a "gliding surface" and the quadriceps with mechanical leverage. A wearing away or softening of the back surface of the patella known as chondromalacia is a painful condition common among young dancers, particularly those engaged in ballet. Dancers who force turnout are predisposed to the

Position of the kneecap when the joint is flexed (bent).

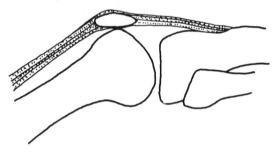

Position of the kneecap when the joint is extended (straight).

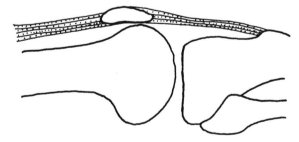

condition, as are those who have "kneecap instability," which, generally, is due to a weakened quadriceps mechanism or, more seriously, to a pathological condition in which the kneecap is prone to slip out of its groove. Occasionally, a genetic abnormality known as a *synovial*

NORMAL ANATOMICAL POSITION OF THE PATELLA

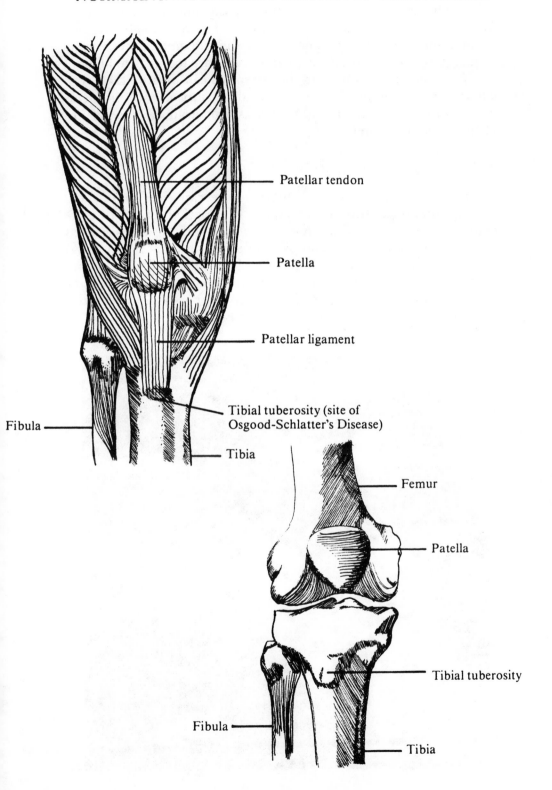

Patellar tendon

Patella

Patellar ligament

Tibial tuberosity (site of
Osgood-Schlatter's Disease)

Fibula

Tibia

Femur

Patella

Tibial tuberosity

Fibula

Tibia

plica—an extra band of tissue at the knee joint—may be the culprit.

You must concentrate on strengthening the inner thigh muscles to stabilize the kneecap. Remember, also, that a weak thigh extensor mechanism can result in overwork of the calf muscles, especially during jumps and leaps; if the thigh muscles are too weak to lift you, *something* must raise you up in the air, so the calf muscles take over. Therefore, a weak quadriceps may lead not just to knee problems but also to Achilles tendinitis as well as foot strain because of improper weight transfer.

Diagnosis

Pain is felt directly above or behind the kneecap when it is pushed. Usually you notice stiffness in the joint after periods of rest or inactivity, sometimes even after *sitting* for a period with the knees crossed or bent. Pain frequently accompanies full extension (straightening) of the knee. Discomfort is experienced both in climbing and going down stairs or from kneeling directly on the kneecap. If the condition is ignored or goes untreated, the pain will persist as the deterioration of the back of the kneecap continues.

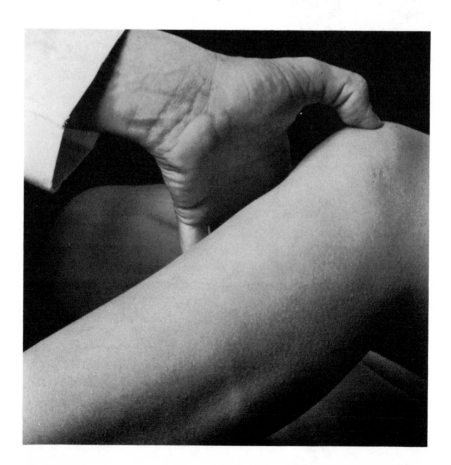

PATELLA STRAPPING

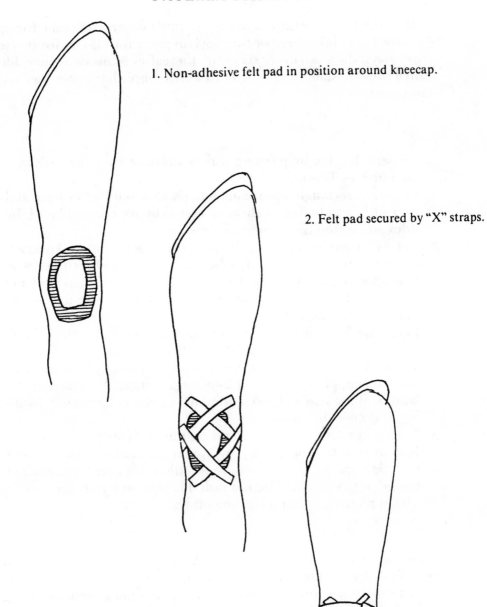

1. Non-adhesive felt pad in position around kneecap.

2. Felt pad secured by "X" straps.

3. Anchor straps are positioned above and below the kneecap.

Ice the knee three times a day for twenty minutes each time for up to three days. Take three or four aspirin every four hours for two to three days, then two every six hours thereafter as needed. For additional comfort stabilize the kneecap with a simple horseshoe pad and strapping.

1. Prepare the skin by painting with benzoin or spraying with pre-tape such as Tuf-Skin.
2. Cut out a rectangle approximately six to seven inches long and four inches wide from a sheet of non-adhesive felt and bevel the sides and round the corners slightly.
3. Cut a hole in the center of the pad just larger than the kneecap. One way this may be accomplished with a degree of accuracy is by first outlining the kneecap with a felt-tipped pen, then pressing the pad against the area as quickly as possible in order to transfer the outline to the felt.
4. Bend the knee just slightly by placing a two-inch thick book under the heel of the leg being taped. Position your felt pad around the kneecap and secure at the top with an "X" formed by two crossing pieces of 1½- or 2-inch elastic tape. Next, secure the bottom of the pad with two additional strips of elastic tape, forming a "double-X" pattern.
5. Anchor the "double-X" top and bottom with strips of three- or four-inch cloth tape that are wrapped circumferentially around the thigh and leg respectively, proceeding from the back, around the sides, to the front. Do not pull this tape on tightly but simply *wrap* it around so that it lays smoothly.

Over the next several weeks, as the healing process proceeds, you may find that additional relief is obtained from wearing an elastic knee brace over your strapping. Try it, and if it helps, wear it during periods of light activity to support further the pad and strapping. Finally, do not return to class too soon; if you do, you will undo the progress that you've made. Listen to your body! It will tell you when it's time to begin dancing again.

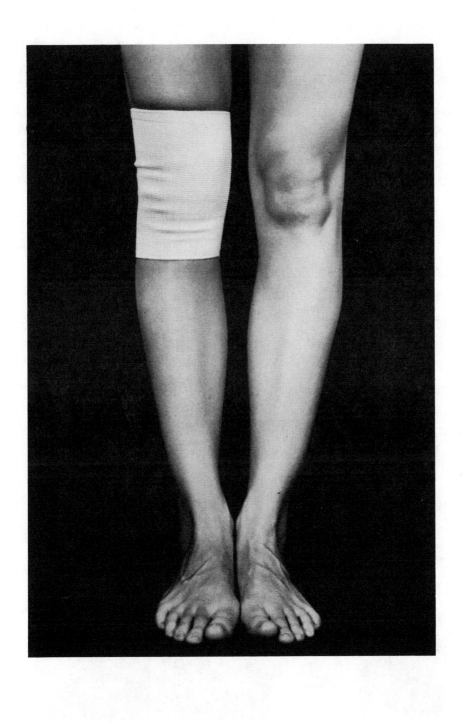

OSGOOD-SCHLATTER'S DISEASE

Osgood-Schlatter's disease (which actually is not a *disease* at all) is a tearing away of the patellar (kneejerk) ligament from its insertion into the tibial tuberosity. It occurs most commonly in young dancers, ages ten through late teens. This predisposition among the younger dancers is due to the fact that the point to which the ligament attaches is not yet hard bone and is easily irritated. Leaps and jumps especially contribute to the onset of Osgood-Schlatter's disease. A fair sized lump will form on the upper leg, at the tibial tuberosity, but this prominence should not be confused with the tibial tuberosity itself, which is normally raised and a little irregular in contour. If you are suffering from this painful condition, the entire area around the tibial tuberosity will be quite enlarged.

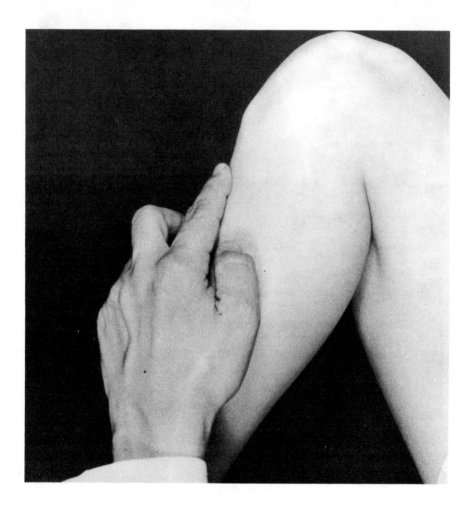

Diagnosis

The pain you experience is directly at the tibial tuberosity, over the attachment of the patellar ligament. At first it is not too severe, more of the nagging variety of discomfort. After a time, however, usually two or three weeks from onset, you will notice the pain when you first get up in the morning. It intensifies with activity rather than abates. Your endurance is reduced, and you experience pain when climbing stairs or squatting. *Pliés* are particularly painful. The area over the tibial tuberosity is quite swollen and tender, and extension of the leg against resistance is difficult to perform comfortably.

Treatment

The only cure for Osgood-Schlatter's disease is *lots of rest,* at least two to three weeks of it. You can deal effectively with the swelling by icing the area three times a day for up to twenty minutes at a time. Take aspirin to reduce the inflammation, three or four every four hours for three days, two every four hours thereafter as needed. (Young dancers should consult their family physician about the use of aspirin.) Remember, all symptoms will disappear with rest alone. *Note:* A permanent reminder of your Osgood-Schlatter's may persist in the form of an enlarged tibial tuberosity, but it is not painful in and of itself.

"HOUSEMAID'S KNEE" OR SWOLLEN KNEECAP
(Prepatella Bursitis)

There is a protective bursa that lies between the kneecap and the skin. Constant, unrelenting impact from falls, particularly in modern dance, irritates this bursa, and it becomes inflamed and distended with synovial fluid. The swelling usually develops over a two or three day period. What starts out as mild pain becomes more severe as the swelling increases. It is not uncommon, in fact, for a prepatella bursa to swell to the size of an egg. You notice swelling over the kneecap, and a sharp pain is produced with movement, especially any form of squatting or kneeling.

Treatment

You should ice the knee for at least twenty minutes three times a day for up to three days. Take three or four aspirin every four hours for three days to reduce the inflammation, two every four hours

HOUSEMAID'S KNEE

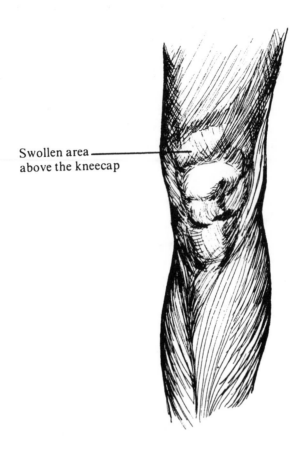

Swollen area
above the kneecap

thereafter as needed. If the pain and swelling have not reduced significantly after three or four days, your orthopedist may have to draw off some of the fluid. You may find that wearing some sort of compression bandage—an elastic knee brace, elastic wrap, or Ace bandage—will assist in evacuating fluid from the area. Keep the knee elevated when you are at rest!

DANCER'S KNEE

Surrounding the knee joint is a sleeve or capsule that is subject to the stress and strain of repeated jumps or leaps. Dancers with very high or very low arches or feet that roll in (pronate) are especially predisposed to this aggravating condition. Rolling or sickling also

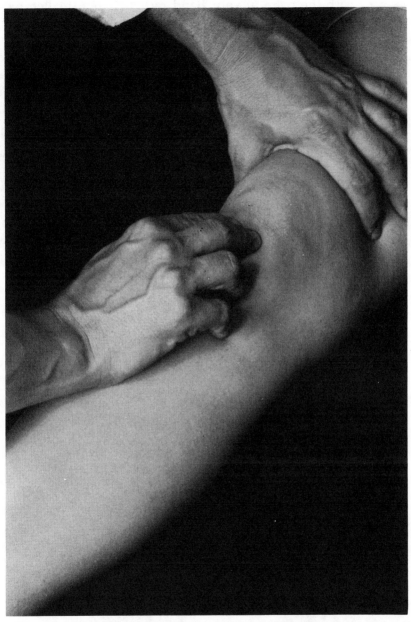

predisposes you to dancer's knee, so you should take care to improve your technique. At first the pain is usually dull or aching, but after a time it becomes sharp and stabbing.

Diagnosis

When asked "Where does it hurt?" you are likely to indicate a large area with the palm of your hand rather than a smaller, more specific one with your finger tip. Lie down on a table or on the floor and lock the knee joint of the affected leg by straightening it. Have a friend squeeze the thigh just above the knee joint and push upwards on the kneecap at the same time. If this simple test produces an area of pain, then it is likely that you have dancer's knee.

Treatment

The best, indeed the *only* treatment for dancer's knee is complete rest. You may deal with the swelling and inflammation by icing the knee three times a day for twenty minutes each time for a period of up to a week. Take three or four aspirin every four hours for up to three days, two every four hours thereafter as needed. Support the knee with an elastic knee brace; this will also help reduce the swelling by gently squeezing out any fluid accumulation. If you begin class too soon, the discomfort will recur, so don't rush things.

JUMPER'S KNEE

Male dancers are especially prone to a condition known as "jump-

JUMPER'S KNEE

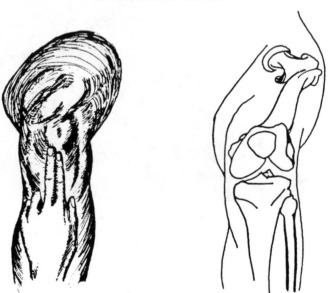

Pain is elicited by pressing against the lower aspect of the kneecap.

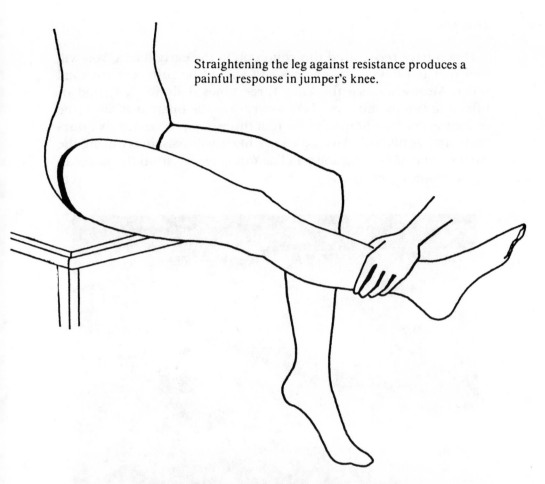

Straightening the leg against resistance produces a painful response in jumper's knee.

er's knee." It develops over a two or three week period as the result of the repetitive shock of jumping. If your arches are extremely high or low, you are more apt to develop this painful condition. The patellar ligament becomes irritated at the point where it attaches to the kneecap. Squatting or jumping becomes quite painful once jumper's knee has set in.

Diagnosis

Sit on the edge of a table or a bed with your knee flexed (bent). Press directly at the point where the patellar ligament inserts into the kneecap. A sharp pain will probably result from the pressure. Next, extend (straighten) the knee against resistance; this also produces a degree of discomfort. Usually there is some inflammation and swelling present.

Treatment

If you have recognized this condition in the early stages, you will find that ten days to two weeks rest should be sufficient for total relief. Meanwhile, ice the knee three times daily for a period of fifteen to twenty minutes. Take aspirin for the inflammation, three or four every four hours for the first three days, two every six hours thereafter as needed. An elastic knee brace will assist in reducing the swelling and stabilizing the patella. You may also strap the kneecap in the following manner.

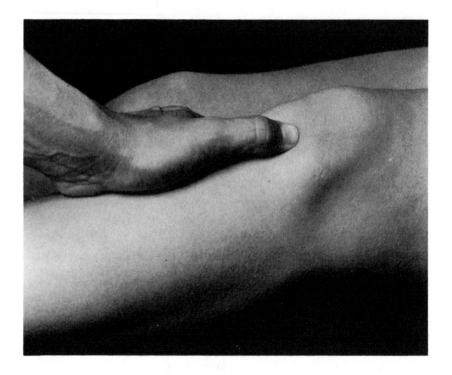

1. Prepare the skin by painting with benzoin or spraying with pre-tape such as Tuf-Skin.
2. Stand erect or lie on a table with the knee extended. Cut four strips of 1- or 1½-inch cloth tape, each one approximately five to six inches long. The strips will be placed around the kneecap in a diamond fashion.
3. The first strip should run from the inside out, crossing just above the kneecap but without touching it.

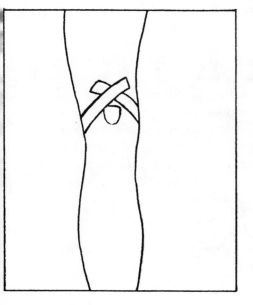

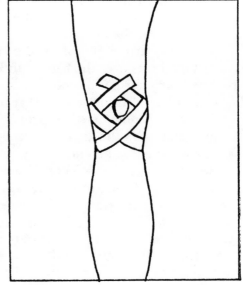

1. The first two strips of tape form an "X" over the kneecap.

2. The second set of strips form an "X" below the kneecap.

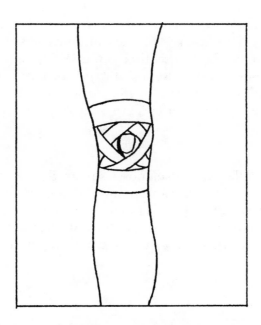

3. Anchor straps in place.

4. Place the second strip of tape in the corresponding position on the other side, so that it is pulled on outside in. An "X" is formed directly over the kneecap.
5. The third strip is run below the kneecap, from the outside in, so that it crosses over the base of the first strip.
6. The fourth strip is placed correspondingly on the other side and is positioned inside out, so that it crosses over the second strip. The knee is now "X-ed" top and bottom, but none of the strips is in contact with the kneecap itself.
7. Finally, anchor the ends of the four strips top and bottom with two-inch tape. *Note:* These last strips must be applied without pressure and laid around the lower thigh and upper leg, front to back, where they cross.

You will find that further support is provided by an elastic knee brace that is worn over the X-strapping.

SUBLUXED PATELLA

If you have a kneecap that chronically "goes out of place," then you may have a condition known as subluxed patella. Subluxed patella is more common among female dancers than male and may be the result of a congenitally shallow groove into which the patella rests, or it may develop over a period of time owing to poor muscle tone and imbalance in the quadriceps muscle. A subluxation occurs not uncommonly during a series of *piqué* turns if the knee is not turned out and over the foot for the *plié.* In fact, the dancer with a subluxed patella notices that *pliés* are quite painful.

Diagnosis

With your leg flat on a table, muscles relaxed, move your kneecap from side to side. If you are able to move it more than one-half inch in either direction, then there is too much laxity. And if the kneecap can be moved more than one inch to the outside, then there is a very good chance that when your quadriceps contracts your patella will sublux.

Treatment

First, it is always a good idea to determine if the quadriceps mechanism is weak or out of balance with the hamstring. Ideally, the dancer should have a strength ratio of three-to-two, quads to

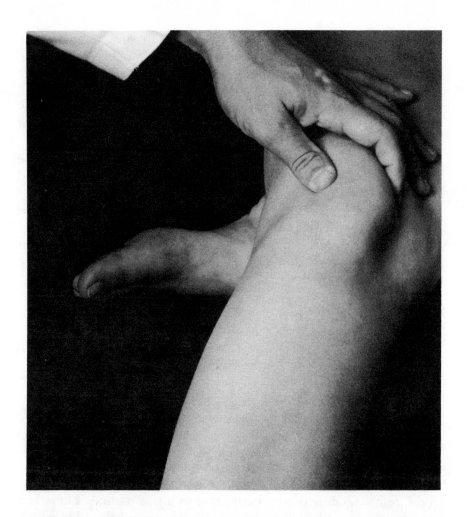

hamstrings. You can test this simply yourself by acquiring a ten-pound bag of flour, placing it in a bookbag or pocketbook, and securing it to your ankle. Extend the leg fully, then lower it. You should do as many of these straight leg lifts as possible, keeping count, of course. Next, lying on the end of your bed, see how many lifts you can do using your hamstrings. Calculate the ratio of strength. If it is greatly disproportionate, that is, significantly out of the three to two relationship, with the hamstrings largely on the strong side, then there is a good chance that by exercising the quads to strengthen them you can stabilize the kneecap and prevent it from "going out."

In the meantime you can keep the kneecap in place by strapping it and supporting its outer side with felt. If the knee continues to "go out," however, you must not hesitate to seek an orthopedist's opinion and advice.

1. Prepare the skin by painting with benzoin or spraying with pre-tape such as Tuf-Skin. For male dancers it may be necessary to shave the area approximately five inches above and below the knee.
2. Cut a shallow C-shaped pad from eighth- or quarter-inch adhesive-backed felt and attach it to the *outside* of the knee so that it just envelops the kneecap.
3. Cut four seven- to nine-inch strips of cloth or elastic tape. The first two strips are applied in such a way that an "X" is formed over the kneecap without coming into contact with its edges.
4. The second set of tape strips are applied to form an "X" below the kneecap and overlap the lower ends of the upper set.
5. Anchor straps of two-inch cloth tape are placed over the ends of the 1½-inch strips, above and below. Wear an elastic knee brace for additional stability.

Remember, proper technique and rehabilitative measures are essential, so do not hesitate to seek professional help if you need it.

PES ANSERINUS BURSITIS
(Pain at the Back of the Knee)

The three hamstring muscles that flex (bend) the leg insert into the tibia at its uppermost rear aspect. The shape that the tendons of the hamstrings take on at this point reminded ancient anatomists of a goose foot—*pes anserinus* in Latin, and so it was named. There is a large bursa located between the pes anserinus and the tibia which facilitates the movement of the hamstring tendons when the knee is either flexed or extended. No clear set of traumatic circumstances can be identified which causes this bursa to become inflamed, but when it does, the pain can be quite disabling. Sometimes, in the early stages especially, you are able to "dance through" the discomfort, but after activity has ceased and you begin to cool down, the pain becomes much worse.

Diagnosis

You notice an aching pain at the back inner side of the knee and around the head (top) of the tibia. Leaps and jumps intensify the discomfort. There is swelling at the back of the knee joint due to inflammation, and bending the knee against resistance causes pain.

RESTRICTION OF SUBLUXING PATELLA

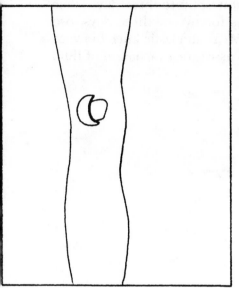

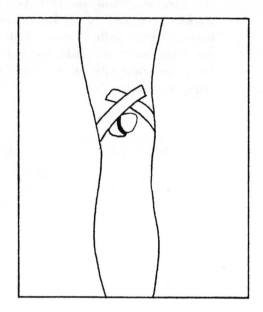

dhesive felt pad is attached on the outer side of
kneecap, along its border.

2. First set of tape straps form an "X" above the
kneecap.

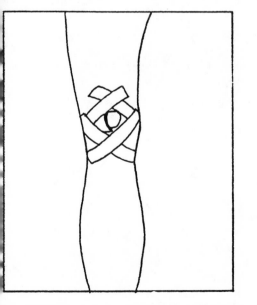

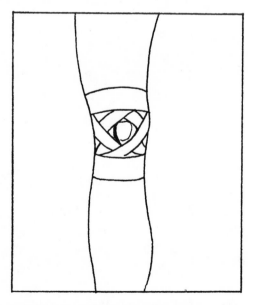

. Second set of straps form an "X" below the
neecap.

4. Position of anchor straps above and below the
knee.

Treatment

Complete rest is necessary in most cases for symptomatic relief from pes anserinus bursitis. You can deal with the swelling with ice packs, three times daily for twenty minutes, up to three days. Take three or four aspirin every four hours for two or three days, two every six hours thereafter as needed. Wear an elastic knee brace or wrap the knee with an Ace bandage to assist the evacuation of fluid from the area.

4

Thigh and Hips

CONTUSIONS AND BRUISES

A VIOLENT BLOW TO ANY PART OF THE BODY, ESPECIALLY TO THE FOOT and leg, which does not break the skin but causes limitation of motion, muscle spasm, swelling, and discoloration, is known as a contusion. The area of injury is quite sensitive to pressure. Dancers usually notice that if they keep moving after a fall or being struck the pain is kept to a minimum. Only after they stop dancing does it become more intense. Thus it is a good idea to keep the part warm and moving to disperse the accumulation of blood in the area. *Note:* Where nerves are more exposed—at the elbow ("funny bone") or head of the fibula on the outside of the leg, for instance—a direct blow can cause either numbness or pain along the length of exposed nerve. This pain may be fleeting in duration or could last for hours. Temporary loss of movement in the part may result as well as the feeling of "pins and needles."

Diagnosis and Treatment

Depending upon the severity of the contusion—first, second, or third degree, follow these procedures, as outlined by Dr. Daniel Arnheim and others.

197

MUSCLES AT THE FRONT OF THE THIGH
(after Barscay's *Anatomy*)

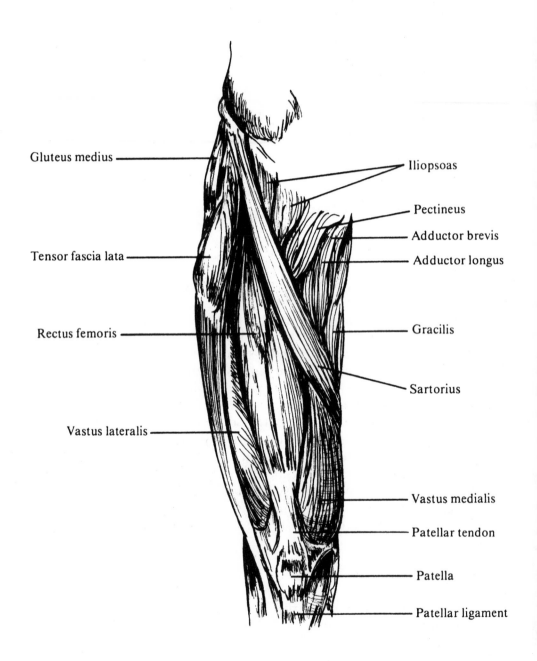

Gluteus medius

Iliopsoas

Pectineus

Adductor brevis

Tensor fascia lata

Adductor longus

Rectus femoris

Gracilis

Sartorius

Vastus lateralis

Vastus medialis

Patellar tendon

Patella

Patellar ligament

FIRST DEGREE

You experience only mild pain and discomfort, with some muscle spasm but little inflammation. Apply a cold pack to the area as soon as possible, leaving it in place for up to a half hour. Next, apply a compression bandage—elastic or Ace—for six to twelve hours depending upon the degree of swelling present. Gradual stretching of the muscle or muscle group involved will help allay the spasms. You should be able to return to class within twenty-four hours.

SECOND DEGREE

Swelling usually comes on very quickly and is accompanied by moderate muscle spasm. The area is painful to the touch, and you will notice some discoloration within the first twenty-four hours. Ice the area for twenty minutes at least three times during the first day or so after sustaining the injury. Elevation will help disperse any fluid accumulation. A compression bandage, Ace or other elastic-type, also will assist in dispersing any fluid accumulation. Muscle spasm can be effectively controlled if you are able to keep the part in an extended (stretched or straightened) position for up to an hour. After seventy-two hours you should begin warm water soaks, whirl-pool if available, for fifteen to twenty minutes twice a day. Begin a program of gradual stretching of the part just as soon as you are able.

THIRD DEGREE

A severe fall or a particularly violent blow not only produces rapid swelling but also brings on severe muscle spasm and loss of function. As with a second degree contusion, ice the part for twenty minutes, three or four times during the first twenty-four hours. Keep the affected part elevated as often as you are able. If it is determined that the muscle has not been torn, or its sheath ruptured, you may begin a program of gradual stretching after twenty-four hours. This stretching should be done in conjunction with warm water soaks or whirlpool, twice daily for fifteen to twenty minutes. As with other contusions you should wear some sort of compression bandage to assist in fluid dispersal and for general comfort.

A "charleyhorse" is a special type of contusion that results from a direct blow to the thigh. There is no break in the skin, so blood accumulates beneath its surface. If the skin on the thigh only is involved a black-blue bruise will probably appear. If, however, deeper tissues are involved—fat, muscles, even bone—then in addition to the surface bruise there may also be a hematoma or blood clot that forms beneath. Muscle spasm and some swelling are present. Discomfort usually does not occur for two or three hours, sometimes even up to six or more. Eventually, however, as blood accumulates beneath the skin, the site of injury becomes quite painful, and you notice a degree of stiffness and muscle spasm. You find it difficult to bend or straighten the knee.

If you think that you have sustained an injury of this sort, do not hesitate to begin your treatment immediately. Do not wait three to six hours for the pain to alert you. Ice the area for twenty to thirty minutes immediately, then twenty minutes three times daily for the next several days. Use crutches if the contusion is so severe that you cannot bear weight on the affected limb. After forty-eight to seventy-two hours begin a regimen of heat, preferably whirlpool or hydrocollator pads, for up to a week or more. Remember, if only the skin is involved, no deeper tissues, you still should not take class for three to four days. The area might otherwise be reinjured and fresh bleeding will occur. If the blow or fall has affected deeper tissues on the front of the thigh, do not plan to return to class for at least two weeks or more. A thigh cuff may also provide additional support and should be worn as needed.

HAMSTRING STRAINS

The powerful hamstring muscles, located at the back of the thigh, are responsible for flexing (bending) the leg at the knee. These muscles may be pulled or strained, torn partially or completely, as the result of a particularly violent or uncoordianted contraction, especially if the dancer has not warmed up sufficiently or has just started back after a long layoff. Also, the failure to put a muscle through its full range of motion predisposes to this sort of injury. Finally, a muscular imbalance between the quadriceps, the muscles on the front of the thigh that straighten the leg, and the hamstrings—normally at a functional strength ratio of three to two, quads to hamstrings—may bring on strain in either muscle group. *Note:* Muscles that cross more than one joint, the hamstrings, for instance, particularly the semimembranosus on the inner back aspect of the thigh, or the triceps surae (collective name for the muscles that form the calf), or the quadriceps on the front of the thigh, especially the rectus femoris, are much more susceptible to strain than those muscles or muscle groups that cross only one joint.

MUSCLES AT THE BACK OF THE THIGH
(After Barcsay's *Anatomy*)

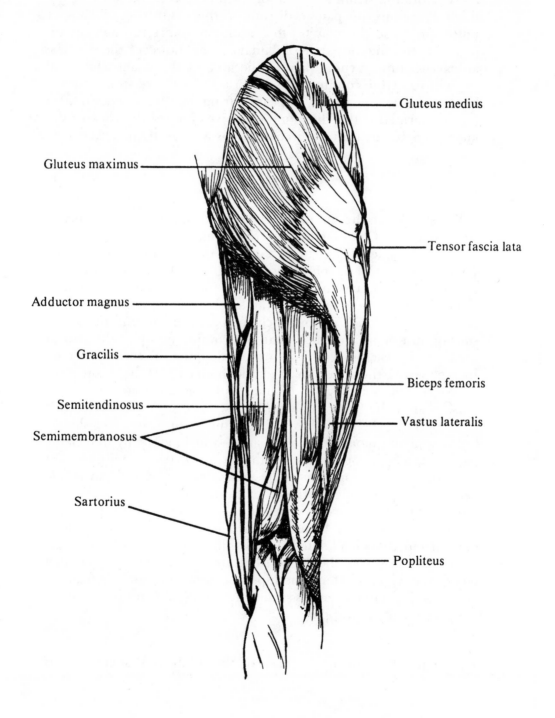

Gluteus medius

Gluteus maximus

Tensor fascia lata

Adductor magnus

Gracilis

Biceps femoris

Semitendinosus

Vastus lateralis

Semimembranosus

Sartorius

Popliteus

Diagnosis

You usually know when you have strained a hamstring because there is often a definite feeling of a rip or tear at the back of the thigh. Preceding any pain or discomfort there is usually a feeling of unsteadiness, so you may try to continue to dance through the injury, not realizing the extent of damage. Soon, however, there will be an excruciating burning pain in the area of the strain which will prevent you from continuing. In the case of a severe strain, a large black and blue area usually appears during the recovery period. Do not be alarmed if this discoloration moves toward the back of the knee over the next several weeks; this is a perfectly natural occurrence.

Treatment

You should ice the site of injury *immediately,* for at least twenty to thirty minutes. Continue this ice treatment, twenty minutes on, ten minutes off, at least three times a day for the next forty-eight hours. Icing helps control the bleeding and effusion of fluid that occurs at the site of the injury and also prevents the formation of a painful clot or hematoma. You should wrap an elastic compression bandage (such as a three-inch or four-inch Ace) securely around the thigh, starting just below the knee joint and continuing up to the fold of the buttocks, each succeeding turn overlapping the former by one-half, or secure the area with an elastic thigh cuff. If the strain is not so severe, begin a program of mild and gradual stretching of the muscles after the first forty-eight hours. Also, after the forty-eight-hour period, when you have discontinued the icing, you should begin applying moist heat to the area—whirlpool or hydrocollator pads, if available, or a moist heating pad, for twenty minutes at a time, three times daily. Keep the area compressed with an elastic bandage the remainder of the time; this not only helps disperse any fluid that may have accumulated in the area but also supports the strained muscle fibers. If the strain is fairly minor, you may be able to return to class on a limited basis within twenty-four to forty-eight hours. In class you should concentrate on movements that flex (bend) the leg and extend the hip—for instance, *passé* to *attitude* to *arabesque.* For a more serious strain you should obtain extra support from a hamstring strapping.

1. Prepare the skin on the back of the thigh by shaving first, if

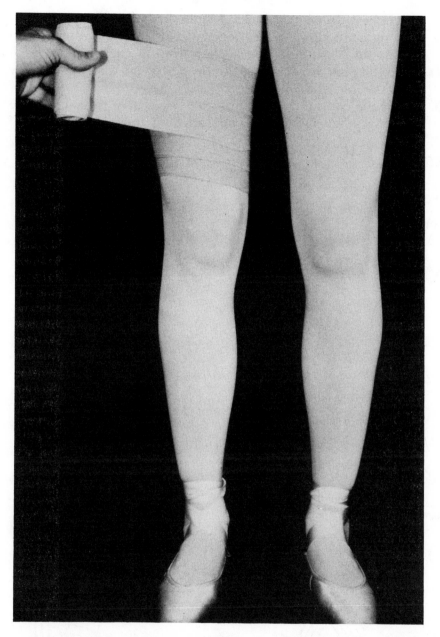

necessary, then painting with benzoin or spraying with pretape such as Tuf-Skin.

2. Place a medium-sized book (1- or 1½-inches thick) under the heel in order to flex the knee at a fifteen- to twenty-degree angle.

3. Place two anchor straps of 1½- or 2-inch cloth tape along the inside and outside of the thigh, running them from a point just

above the knee joint to the level of the fold of the buttock.

4. Starting at the lower (knee) end, place strips of two-inch cloth tape in an X-pattern from anchor strap to anchor strap, each succeeding one overlapping the former by one-half, all the way up to the fold of the buttock.

5. Secure the ends of the X-straps with two-inch or three-inch tape that runs parallel to your original anchor straps.

HAMSTRING STRAIN STRAPPING

1. Heel rests on book to flex knee; outer anchor strap in position.

2. First set of "X" straps in position on back of thigh.

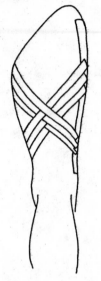

3. Three sets of "X" straps in position.

4. "X" strapping is anchored from the knee to the fold of the buttocks; first strap in place just above the knee.

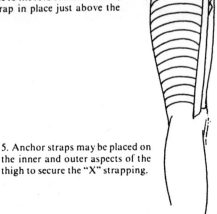

5. Anchor straps may be placed on the inner and outer aspects of the thigh to secure the "X" strapping.

6. Finally, secure the thigh further by wrapping it with an Ace or other elastic bandage from knee to buttocks (as described above). A thigh cuff works especially well.

Do not resume classes until the muscle is completely healed. There is a very great risk of reinjury to the vulnerable and weakened muscle tissue.

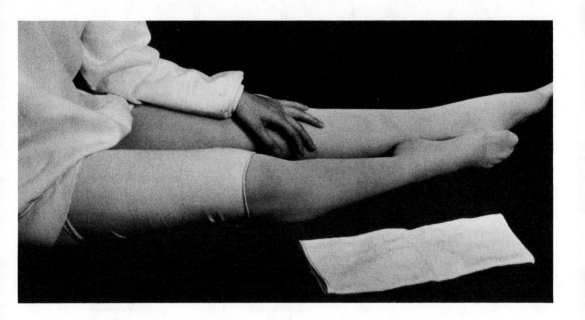

QUADRICEPS STRAINS

A strain of the quadriceps muscle can be brought on either by a sudden violent contraction of the muscle mechanism or, simply, by what is known as a "static muscle contraction," when the muscle is held stationary in a bent position and abnormal stress is placed along its length. Quadriceps strains are more common among female dancers than male.

Diagnosis

As with hamstring strains you will feel a ripping or tearing sensation, perhaps even a "giving way" of the muscle. You usually are not aware of the degree of injury for several hours, but when the pain comes on, it is intense and usually accompanied by spasm and swelling. The injured area fills with blood and lymph fluid from the torn vessels, making it quite difficult to bend your knee.

TAPING A STRAINED QUADRICEPS

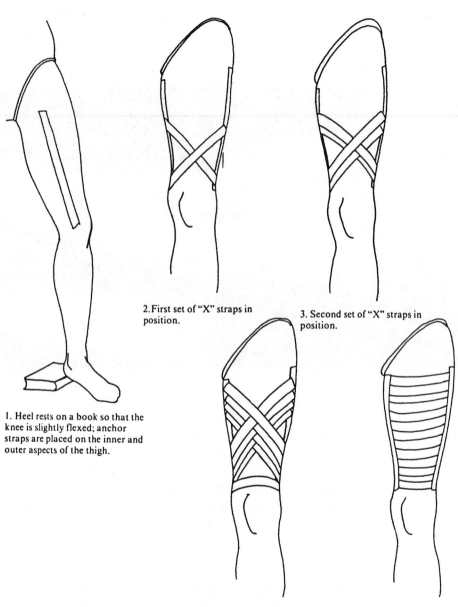

1. Heel rests on a book so that the knee is slightly flexed; anchor straps are placed on the inner and outer aspects of the thigh.

2. First set of "X" straps in position.

3. Second set of "X" straps in position.

4. After the thigh has been "X-ed," wrap it from the knee up to the fold of the buttock with an elastic bandage.

5. Secure the inner and outer sides of the thigh with anchor straps.

Treatment

The treatment is identical to a hamstring strain except the supportive strapping is applied to the *front* of the thigh rather than to the back of it. (See "Hamstring Strains" for instructions on therapeutic measures: ice, heat, and so on.)

1. Prepare the skin on the front of the thigh by shaving first, if necessary, then painting with benzoin or spraying with pretape such as Tuf-Skin.
2. Place a medium-sized book (1- or 1½-inches thick) under the heel in order to flex the knee at a fifteen to twenty-degree angle.
3. Place two anchor straps of 1½- or 2-inch cloth tape along the inside and outside of the thigh, running them from a point just above the knee joint to the level of the fold of the buttock.
4. Starting at the lower (knee) end, place strips of two-inch cloth tape in an X-pattern from anchor strap to anchor strap, each

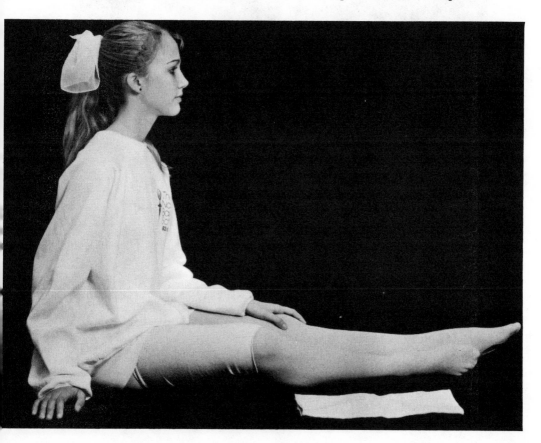

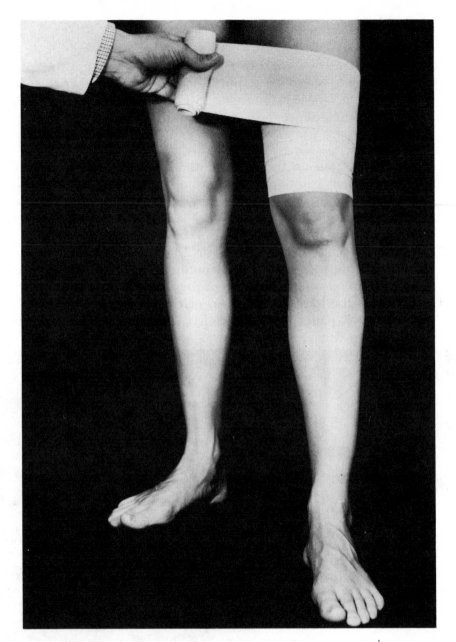

succeeding one overlapping the former by one-half, all the way up to the fold of the buttock.

5. Secure the ends of the X-straps with two- or three-inch tape that runs parallel to your original anchor straps.

6. Finally, secure the thigh further by wrapping it with an Ace or other elastic bandage from knee to buttocks (as described above). An elastic thigh cuff works especially well.

Again, the risk of reinjury is very great, so do not resume class or performance until the muscle has healed entirely. You may find that continuing with the elastic support, even after you have stopped taping the thigh, will give you an increased sense of security.

SHORT LEG SYNDROME AND IMBALANCE

Often a dancer notices that balancing on one leg or the other produces a rocking motion, making balance difficult to accomplish. All other factors equal—that is, muscle balance and tone are normal, there is no sign of scoliosis, you are not fatigued, and so on—then a short leg may be at the base of the problem. Here is a quick test that is easy to perform.

Lie flat on your back, completely relaxed, hands by your sides. Have a partner grasp your ankles from beneath and pull your legs rather forcibly four or five times. Press the inner ankle bones (medial malleoli) together and observe their position: if your legs are equal in length the bones should meet at the same level. If, however, one appears higher than the other, then it is very likely that one of your legs is shorter than the other.

Next you will want to determine the anatomical basis for the short leg, whether it is due to pelvic tilt, differing tibial or femoral lengths, unilateral pronation, and so on.

Sit in a straight back chair on a level floor, shoes and socks off, feet placed firmly on the floor. Place a carpenter's level across your knees. The bubble will be centered if both legs are the same length. Any discrepancy in tibial lengths will cause the bubble to move to one side or the other.

Another way to determine relative leg length is with the simple Deerfield Test. You should wear flat tennis or jogging shoes for this test because the rounded aspect of the heel makes observation less accurate.

Lie flat on your stomach on a table with your feet and ankles extended over the edge. Have a partner flex both ankles to a right angle, which you will hold. As you lie there, he can easily observe which if either of the legs is short. Now flex both knees at a ninety-degree angle, keeping the ankles at a ninety-degree angle as well. If there is an anatomical variation, then your

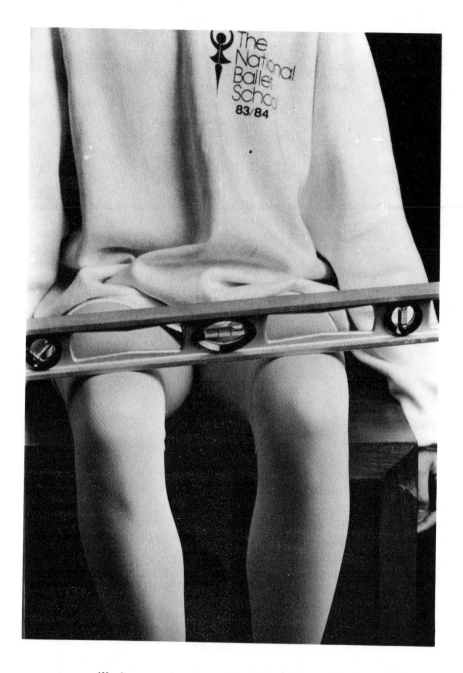

partner will observe the same discrepancy in this position. If, on the other hand, both legs appear to be the same length, then you have what is known as a "functional shortness" of one leg. That is, the short leg compensates for itself by adjusting to the discrepancy.

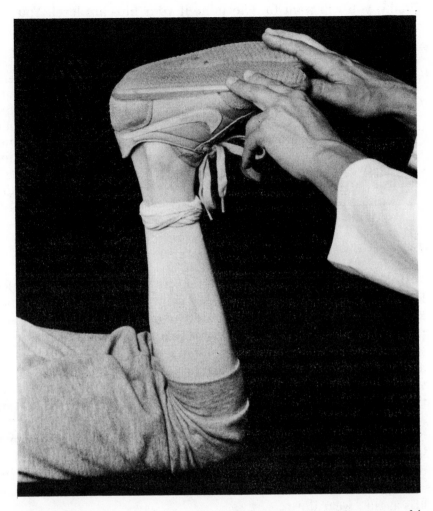

To measure the actual length of a limb from hip to ankle, proceed in this manner:

Press along the front aspect of the hip until you locate the point that juts out farthest, marking its position on each side of the hip with a felt-tipped pen. Next mark identical points on both inner ankle bones. Using a cloth tape, measure and record the distance between the hip and inner ankle bone on both sides. You should take at least three or four measurements, as there will likely be some slight variation in your figures (you should not be more than an eighth of an inch out on either side). Go with the two or three measurements that are equal. Remember, while your partner takes these measurements you must be perfectly *relaxed*, hands by your sides.

Finally, you will want to determine if your hips are level. You will need a partner to assist you.

Begin by using the points on the front of the hips that you marked for your leg length measurements. Have your friend hold a string between these two points. The string should be level if the front aspect of the pelvis is level. Next, check your hips from the rear. You will observe a dimple over each buttock, near the spine. Mark these dimples with your pen. Your partner will then mark the uppermost flares of the hip bones by outlining two or three inches on each, being certain the same anatomical parts are marked on both sides. Connect each set of points with a ruler or carpenter's level. They should be level; a dip to one side or the other indicates posterior pelvic tilt.

Treatment

If after applying these tests, you determine that you do have a leg length discrepancy, you will find that you can improve your balance and, at the same time, avoid a number of troublesome aches and pains, by inserting a heel lift of felt or foam rubber in the shoe of the shorter leg. Remember, an eighth-inch leg length discrepancy is not at all unusual, nor is a quarter-inch difference likely to prove troublesome. However, if you are out three-eighths to one-half inch, then you must try to restore balance with a heel lift. Begin by adding an eighth-inch lift only; if this amount is insufficient, add another eighth-inch lift. Most dancers find that they can add an eighth-inch lift to the heels of their pointe shoes without difficulty or interference, but more than a quarter-inch lift seems to annoy them by raising the heel too high out of the shoe. You can replace felt heel lifts as they wear down.

Remember, more than balance may be upset by a short leg. You could develop a tendency to pull the same muscle or strain the same muscle groups over and again. Shinsplints and low back pain can often be attributed to the compensatory mechanisms at work when one leg is shorter than the other. Chronic sciatica could also develop. Add the necessary amount of lift to prevent further problems. Here's an easy way to make a heel lift from adhesive felt.

1. Place a square of eighth-inch adhesive-backed felt on the floor and trace your heel on it for a length of three to four inches (depending upon the size of your foot).
2. Cut out the heel pad and bevel down the front to a comfortable angle.

3. Insert into your pointe shoes. If you need more than an eighth-inch lift, attach another layer of felt and bevel.

If, after all your testing and measuring, you determine that the legs are no more than one eighth inch in disparity, but you are still having trouble balancing on one leg, the source of your problem may be a varus attitude *(turned in)* of the foot or leg. You can often adjust this problem by making a felt heel lift as described above, but instead of putting it in your shoe whole, you cut away the *outer half.* Bevel this pad on the inner and front sides and insert on the *inside* of your pointe shoe. This simple device may be all you need to restore your balance. Remember, however, that an eighth-inch lift is usually enough to correct the problem, but some dancers have used as much as a quarter-inch lift.

GROIN STRAIN

The "loose-jointed" dancer who has not taken care to strengthen her groin muscles properly—especially the iliopsas, adductor group, and rectus femoris—is prone to stretch and tear them. These muscles are responsible for dance movements that adduct and inwardly rotate the thigh. And, as for other muscle strains, inadequate stretching or a lack of sufficient warm-up, even general muscle fatigue from overuse, will increase the likelihood of a strain in the groin area. Any or all of these predisposing factors, in conjunction with generally poor muscle tone, may cause a simple strain just from a sudden or violent internal rotation of the thigh or sometimes even of the trunk. Dr. Daniel Arnheim and others have stressed the importance of evaluating the strain to determine first the muscles involved, and second, the extent of damage.

Diagnosis

Even though the movement causing the strain may have been sudden, even fleeting, the pain that results probably will not develop in the area for several hours, sometimes for a period of up to six hours. When it does come on, however, it is usually quite severe, perhaps disabling, causing you difficulty even with the simplest movements. So, before you consider the proper treatment, apply these simple functional tests as soon as possible after the injury to determine which of the groin muscles is involved.

TESTING FOR STRAINED ADDUCTOR MUSCLES

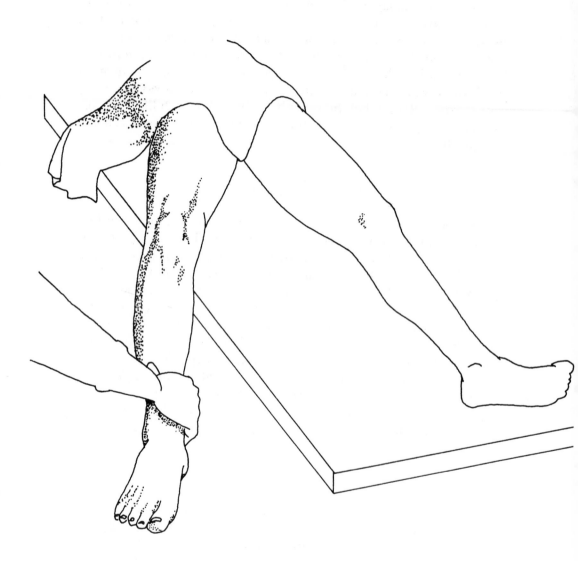

The leg is pulled inward against resistance.

RECTUS FEMORIS

Sit with both legs hanging over the edge of a table. Straighten the affected limb against resistance. Pain in the groin area indicates that you have probably strained the rectus femoris.

ADDUCTOR GROUP

Lie on your back with your thigh abducted (away from your body) as far as possible. Slowly draw it back toward the table against resistance. Pain in the groin indicates that you have probably strained one or more of the adductor muscles.

ILIOPSOAS

Sit with both legs hanging over the edge of the table. Flex (lift) the affected thigh against resistance. Pain from a strained iliopsoas is felt quite deep in the groin area. If you have this type of strain you may have already noticed that you are inclined to stoop a bit at the waist when you walk, and that it is often difficult to stand up straight.

Treatment

It is imperative that you discontinue *all* activity for as long as you possibly can. Remember, if you do not allow a stretched muscle to heal properly—and in general this usually means more than just a two-day rest—the chances are good that you will reinjure the part very quickly. Furthermore, the scar tissue that results from a poorly-healed muscle will predispose you to a new strain. So, ice the area for twenty to thirty minutes, three times a day, for the first forty-eight hours. On the third day you should begin heat therapy, using a whirlpool or hydrocollator pads, if available, or moist heating pads. Ice and heat are essential for assisting repair, regardless of the groin muscles involved.

Finally, you may apply a groin wrap to support the injured muscle and reduce the chances of further injury.

1. Place a wedge of non-adhesive felt or sponge rubber directly over the strained area, keeping the thigh turned *in* while the elastic bandage is applied.
2. Using four- or six-inch elastic wrap, begin at the top of the inner aspect of the thigh, bringing the wrap around the thigh and over the hip at the angle illustrated.

TESTING FOR STRAINED ILIOPSOAS OR ILIOPSOAS BURSITIS

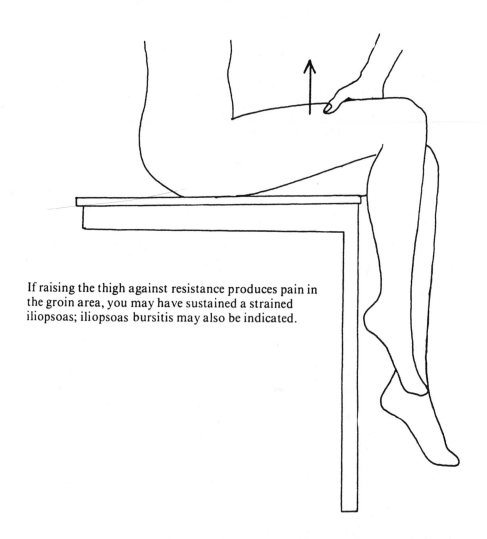

If raising the thigh against resistance produces pain in the groin area, you may have sustained a strained iliopsoas; iliopsoas bursitis may also be indicated.

3. Proceed around the lower abdomen and opposite side of the trunk, then bring the wrap back around to the starting point.
4. Repeat this pattern, overlapping each succeeding turn by approximately two-thirds, until the roll of elastic wrap is all used up.

This groin wrap provides minimal support only; do not overexert until the damaged muscle tissue has completely healed.

GROIN WRAP

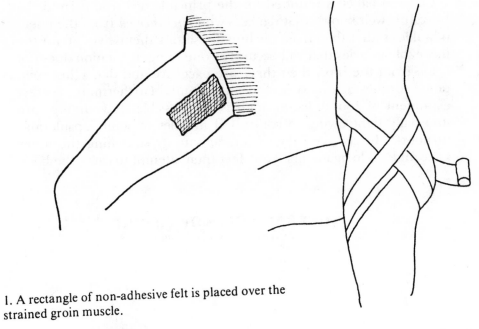

1. A rectangle of non-adhesive felt is placed over the strained groin muscle.

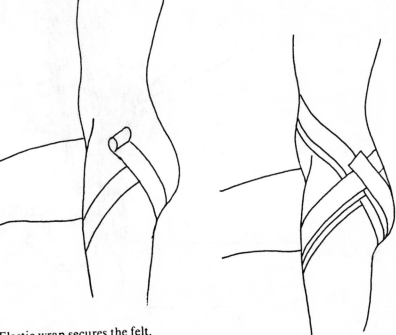

2. Elastic wrap secures the felt.

3. Elastic wrap continued.

4. Elastic wrap in place.

Classical ballet is founded on the principle of turnout from the hips. It is well known that dancers who *force turnout* from the knees or ankles rather than from the hips are setting themselves up for the inevitable injuries that will occur. For one thing, if rotation does not come from the hips, then there are excessive and damaging rotational torques at the knee and ankle joints. Furthermore, correct alignment of foot-to-leg-to-thigh is not possible. If your hips are unusually tight owing to contracted muscles or joint capsule and turnout is forced, you try to compensate by stretching the inner knee and ankle ligaments. Your feet then attempt to carry the body

DEEP MUSCLES OF THE HIP
(after Barcsay's *Anatomy*)

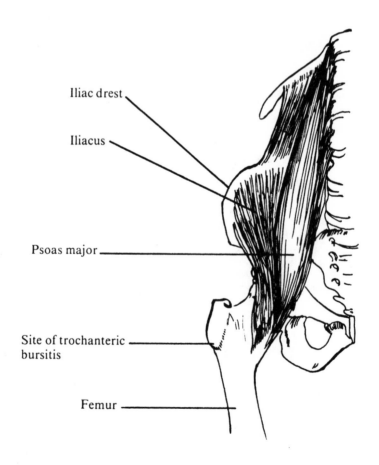

Iliac drest

Iliacus

Psoas major

Site of trochanteric bursitis

Femur

weight and bear the unusual forces that pass them to the inner arches, causing them to turn out, with a subsequent flattening of the arch. Pain then may result not just at the hip level but also on the *inner* side of the foot, ankle, or knee. Additional injuries or problems are then likely to occur: metatarsalgia, plantar fasciitis, stretched or sprained ligaments, and tendinitis or bursitis, among them. Dancers must therefore strive constantly toward the ideal of proper turnout, *turnout from the hips.*

The range of motion you have in your hips is determined by the ligaments that bind the femur (thigh bone) to the pelvis, and even under relatively normal circumstances, this range of motion may not be as much as you expect: about forty-five degrees of abduction, fifteen degrees of extension, and sixty-five degrees of flexion. Assuming the hip joint is anatomically sound, the most common complaint in this area among dancers is inflammation of the large bursae that surround the joint.

Trochanteric Bursitis

Lying between the greater trochanter of the femur and the iliotibial band is a large bursa which may become irritated and inflamed from overexertion or occasionally from direct trauma (a kick or bad fall, for instance). The bursa distends with fluid and becomes rather painful. However, real discomfort comes on over a three to five day period and usually limits most forms of activity, even a simple crossing of the legs. Direct pressure to the area will produce a deep-seated pain.

To determine if you have trochanteric bursitis, lie on your side and abduct the hip (move it *away* from the body). Usually there is a degree of discomfort produced during this activity. Now have a friend try to resist this outward movement of the hip; if you have trochanteric bursitis, the discomfort will greatly increase. Remember, it is when the overlying tissue squeezes the bursa that you experience the pain.

You must discontinue all activity until the symptoms completely subside. Take three or four aspirin every four hours for the first seventy-two hours, two every six hours thereafter, as needed. Ice the area for twenty to thirty minutes, three times daily for three days; heat is recommended thereafter. If you have not noticed a significant degree of relief after four or five days, you should consult an orthopedist.

TESTING FOR TROCHANTERIC BURSITIS

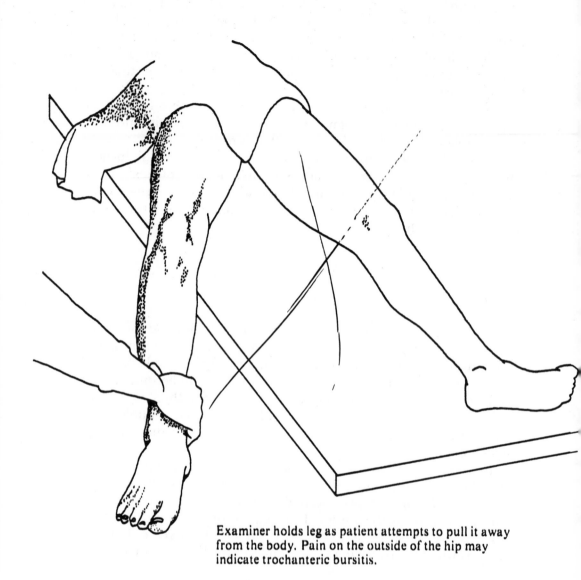

Examiner holds leg as patient attempts to pull it away from the body. Pain on the outside of the hip may indicate trochanteric bursitis.

Iliopsoas Bursitis

The iliopsoas muscle assists the internal and external obturators, superior and inferior gemelli, quadratus femoris, and piriformis in

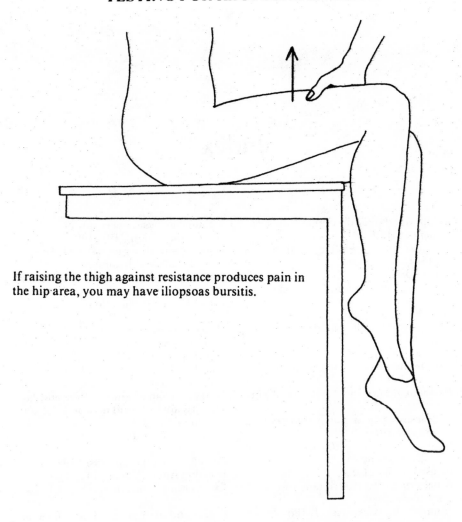

If raising the thigh against resistance produces pain in the hip area, you may have iliopsoas bursitis.

achieving and maintaining turnout. Its principal function is in forcibly flexing (bending) the thigh. Located between the tendon of the iliopsoas muscle and the hip joint is a bursa which, if irritated, produces pain in the front aspect of your hip. It might be interesting for you to know that for dancers, iliopsoas bursitis is about the only problem that can cause pain in this area. Direct trauma to the front of the hip or overexertion of the iliopsoas are the principal sources of irritation. Like trochanteric bursitis, this condition develops over a three to five day period. Pressing the area with your hand or raising the thigh against resistance will produce a painful response. Treatment is identical to that for trochanteric bursitis.

Index

Hammer toes: description and treatment of, 47–49
Hamstring strains, 200, 202–5
Heel, pain in, 111–29
Heel spur, 113, 118–20
Housemaid's knee, 185–86

Ice: therapeutic uses of, 16–17
Icthyol ointment, 53–54
Iliopsoas: strain of, 215–16
Iliopsoas bursitis: testing for, 216, 220–21
Imbalance: and leg length, 209–13
Inferior calcaneal bursitis, 121
Ingrown toenails: description and treatment of, 43–46
Inversion sprain (ankle), 139–45

Jones fracture, 97–100
Jumper's knee, 188–92

Knee, 171–96
Kneecap, 178–85, 192–94

Leg length: measuring, 209–12
Ligaments: knee, 174–78
Low Dye strap, 115–17

Metatarsalgia: description and treatment of, 76–82
Metatarsals (bones): stress fractures of, 82–88
Muscle pulls. See specific muscles

Nerve tumors. See Neuroma
Neuroma (benign nerve tumor): description and treatment of, 71–75

Osgood-Schlatter's disease, 184–85

Pain: in ankle, 137–46; in arch of foot, 89–93; in back of heel, 126–37; in back of leg, 162–70; in ball of foot, 71–88; in great toe joint, 50–60; under great toe joint, 61–65; in groin, 213–16; in heel (underside), 111–25; in hips, 219–21; in inner and outer leg, 147–61; in knee, 171–96; in kneecap, 178–82; in outside of foot, 97–100, 101–5, 105–8; in thigh, 197–209; in top of foot, 94–96, 109–10
Peroneal tendinitis, 65, 158–61
Pes anserinus bursitis, 194, 196
Petit battement: and knee injuries, 174

Petite allegro: and arch pain, 89
Piqué turns: and subluxed patella, 192
Plantar fascia, 111–12
Plantar fasciitis: description and treatment of, 111–18
Plantaris muscle, torn, 169–70
Plantar warts: description and treatment of, 34–40; distinguished from callous, 36
Pliés: and ankle sprains, 139; and arch pain, 89; and bunions, 50; and knee injuries, 172, 173; and metatarsalgia, 76; and subluxed patella, 192
Posterior calcaneal bursitis, 126–29
Posterior tibial shinsplints, 147, 151
Pulled muscles. See specific muscles

Rectus femoris: strain of, 215
Relevé: and Achilles tendinitis, 130; and peroneal tendinitis, 158; and shinsplints, 154
"Rolling in": and bunions, 50; and knee injuries, 172, 186; and plantar fasciitis, 111
"Rolling out": and Achilles tendinitis, 130
Rond de jambe: and knee injuries, 171, 174; and peroneal tendinitis, 158

Saut de basque: and ankle sprains, 139
Sesamoid bones, 52, 61
Sesamoiditis: description and treatment of, 60–63
Shinsplints: description and treatment of, 147–57
Short leg syndrome, 209–13
"Sickling": and knee injuries, 186–87; and peroneal tendinitis, 158; and strained calf muscle, 162
Soleus (muscle), pulled, 166–69
Sprains, ankle, 137–46
Sprains, great toe: description and treatment of, 68–70
Stiffness: in big toe joint, 64–68
Strains: calf muscle, 162–65; groin, 213, 215, 216; hamstring, 200, 202–5; quadriceps, 205–8
Stress fractures: metatarsal, 82–88; tibia, 151
Subluxed cuboid: description and treatment of, 105–8
Subluxed patella: description and treatment of, 192–94